The Future Is BIG

The Future Is BIG

How Emerging Technologies Are Transforming
Industry and Societies

Uma Vanka

BEP

BUSINESS EXPERT PRESS

Leader in applied, concise business books

The Future Is BIG:
How Emerging Technologies Are Transforming Industry and Societies

Copyright © Business Expert Press, LLC, 2024.

Cover design by Charlene Kronstedt

Interior design by Exeter Premedia Services Private Ltd., Chennai, India

First published in 2023 by
Business Expert Press, LLC
222 East 46th Street, New York, NY 10017
www.businessexpertpress.com

ISBN-13: 978-1-63742-491-9 (paperback)
ISBN-13: 978-1-63742-492-6 (e-book)

Business Expert Press Service Systems and Innovations in Business and Society Collection

First edition: 2023

10 9 8 7 6 5 4 3 2 1

To my lovely wife Jessica, daughter Janya, and son Jaivant
who let me sit in the corner and do my thing,
despite the odds.

Description

From the daggers and axes of the cavemen societies to today's spacecraft, self-driving cars, metaverses, and AI-filled societies, technology has significantly emerged and brought about a massive transformation to our lives. The pace of this innovation has been particularly colossal in this industrial era, continuously disrupting our lives. Where will this imminent tech take us in the future? This book will dissect how various aspects of our lives will be transformed in the years to come, with a particular *focus on* **how to benefit from these emerging technologies**. You will gain a 360-degree view by getting a historical perspective of technology since discussions about the future are seldom complete without history.

The ongoing debate on whether technology will replace our jobs in the future is causing great panic. *Technology will not take away our jobs; lack of technology certainly will. This book will provide a freight of the latest tech-driven trends to equip everyone to face the future, like a one-time software upgrade.* Whether you're a freshly graduated student, a bewildered parent, or a tech enthusiast, this book offers everything you need to stay ahead of the game. This book will also help budding entrepreneurs and corporate professionals identify opportunities to incorporate tech into their businesses through a glimpse into the future.

Updating oneself in technology doesn't have to be rocket science. People need a quick sweep of the cutting-edge technologies at the forefront that make a difference in their lives. They want to read that in the easiest language without that overwhelming feeling of graduation. This book *explains the effects of complex topics* such as robotics, blockchain, AI, IoT, VR, XR, AR, cloud, BCI, CRISPR, mRNA, 3D and 4D printing, Web 3.0, and NetZero *in a facile manner that even a tech-illiterate can follow.*

Keywords

books on technology and business; books on technology and future; best books on future technology; best books on technology and society; books on technology innovation; books on technology for dummies; books on technology for nontechnical people; technology scouting books; technology explained; history of technology books; key trends in technology for dummies; technology books for dummies 2022; information technology books; how technology works book; technology history books; how to use technology book; cutting-edge research on technology for beginners; leading in the digital world; tech books for beginners; tech books for dummies; tech books to read; tech books; books on technology and business trends; keeping up with technology for dummies

Contents

Preface

Your reason for choosing this book may be personal or professional. I thank you from my heart's ventricle for picking a book that cares about you and your survival in this techy world. Obscure part to thank someone from? This obscurity is inspired by the fate of millions of people who think technology is not their cup of tea.

However, in the 21st century fast-everything culture, knowledge is broadly available and is profuse than ever but has become masked with layers of meaning that few people understand the important points the creators make. And forget about applying the learned in their life. Most of this knowledge comes from theses and dissertations and do not talk to the minds of a nontechnical person. The discussion is so specific that few people outside the domain can relate, let alone apply in their lives.

As modern technology advanced, the now and here overpowered the yesterday and tomorrow. There's barely a vantage point from where to look at the past, present, and future technologies. We're at the crossroads of the innovative, breathtaking, and spectacular noise hurtled at us continuously. We do not know where the noise is coming from, nor do we know what it means. That's why we need a spot. A spot to get the sense of how big or detailed the web of technology is that integrates our life.

This book is for those who want to read a book on technology but find it too intimidating. I aim to give the readers a wide vantage point and a bit of everything to get started in this convoluted world. While doing so, I might seem to scribble on the surface, barely scratching through, afraid of going to the deep. But that would be nothing more than intentional. I attempt to lure the beginners but not shoo away the mid-rowers.

There are two groups of people in the world: one who understands and uses technology daily and the other who has no idea how technology functions but may have been using it to some to no extent. Topics like artificial intelligence and space technology can quickly put a person to sleep if you start with DDoSes and ballistics. Yet, ordinary citizens are hurled with dozens of techno-keywords every day as if something exciting is cooking that would ease their transition into the job market. Technology has gone from as simple as starting a fire to as complicated as running the Large Hadron Collider. (The Large Hadron Collider is a mammoth machine on earth that accelerates particles at a very high speed only to collide them.)

Learning is akin to night sky watching. With only a quick sweep at the feeble stars, you can narrow down on the interesting ones. That's the *extensive*. You "jack" the extensive—that's your interest gnawing on the available knowledge, expecting to witness more details of the stars. If you're keen enough to zoom through a telescope, you'll see galaxies of stars stuffed in that very single dot. And that's the *intensive*. Without an extensive view of things in your discipline, intensive exercises mean nothing more than drilling a nail into the hardest spot on the wall.

The rationale behind my writing this book is simple. I want the inexperienced and the freshly baked out to revisit simplicity to keep up with the frontlines of bleeding-age technology. I've tried to keep everything simple and authenticate my data and facts through citations from trusted sources. And these sources are not books found in big libraries only the big brains can access. Anyone can instantly access them without even a subscription for the first few visits, at least most of them. Feel free to note these sources—the ones that interest you.

The book is divided into two parts: Chapter 2 and the rest. Chapter 2 is a fictional story that zooms into the life of a character named Falcon and his futuristic world. Based on the day-to-day technologies Falcon uses and experiences, the rest of the chapters extrapolate them into perspective in real life. However, don't sweat on matching every other technology in the story to its corresponding explanation in the book. Not every technology I discuss in Chapter 2 is present in the book and vice versa.

CHAPTER 1

The BIG Beginning

Imagine sitting in a time machine and traveling back in time. Not a year. Not a thousand or a million years. I'm taking you 4.5 billion years back to witness the birth of this beautiful planet Earth we now call home. The journey is long, tiring, and arduous, but let's use the time machine to breeze through the highlights.

While the formation of our planet was an exciting event, all we'll see on our journey is fire and dust gradually settling to form the round ball of natural beauty. This predominantly red ball turns blue and builds its patches of land all over, without any major changes, for the next billion years.

A billion years later, something magical happens: organic life comes into being. The earth's climate goes through its cycles, and species come in and out of existence. However, things are transforming so slowly that no noticeable changes occur over long periods in our time machine journey.

Perhaps the most significant event and arguably the most relevant to us occurs almost another 3.5 billion years later, around 300,000 years ago, through the evolution of modern-day humans (Greshko 2021). The human ancestors change the way the world looks through their superior intelligence. To understand how much they transform this planet, simply take away everything manmade from this world. That puts us back in the caveman's world. While we have the time machine, let's zoom in on this very journey that modern-day humans went through. We start from the hunting society, also called Society 1.0.

Society 1.0: The Hunting Society

Society 1.0 is a primitive society, with people hunting on demand to get their food. They hunt, they feed, and the process repeats. Parents provide for their children and feed them until they can hunt on their own. To save, be saved, and hunt were the daily chores. It's been the same routine day after day for thousands of years.

Only after you've waited for a considerable period on fast-forwarding the journey, you'll get some light, literally. The ancestors master the art of using fire. A major shift in climate, most probably caused by drought and starvation, drives them out of Africa. The concept of a shared society begins, meaning some people hunt and others focus on building houses, making hunting tools, and crafting pottery. They exchange goods and services for survival.

This standard of life persists for over 290,000 years without any noteworthy mention. Think about this for a minute. We are not talking about scores of years or hundreds, not even thousands. No noticeable change was observed in our ancestors' lives for almost 3,000 centuries (Dorey 2021).

Society 2.0: The Farming Society

We start to notice a significant change in our lives starting at around the 290,000-year mark, roughly 10,000 years ago (*National Geographic Society* 2022), through the domestication of plants and animals. Part of it is due to the increasing demand, driven by an increased population and decreased supply because of overhunting. Our ancestors also become a bit smarter and overcome the fate given to them by nature and grow things instead of depending on what is available. This soil-fed society evolves civilizations around the agricultural land and are termed as farming society, or Society 2.0.

Our ancestors are no longer at the mercy of Mother Nature to feed them. They grow their own plants and rear animals. While the most necessities are taken care of, is that enough? Well, that is a small victory over nature; our ancestors in this society are still stuck in their little societies, isolated from everyone. They are still dependent on nature for other essential resources, such as water and light. Even though they grow smarter, they're vulnerable to natural disasters, blood-thirsty animals, and the like. And then, there're again 100 centuries of no prominent evolutionary changes. Sure, civilizations proliferate, languages will be come more complex, agriculture evolves, we figure out ways to use animals and birds as helpers, life expands into other parts of the world, and trading methods improve. If we move a human being from 10,000 years ago into a society from a few 100 years ago, she would have only a limited amount of catching up to do with societal changes.

Society 3.0: The Industrial Society

Suddenly, the quiet, serene world turns into a bustling, rumbling, and rattling cooking space of hot, molten, spinning, giant machine-made items never seen before. We find ourselves in 18th-century Great Britain at the outset of the great Industrial Revolution that later spread like wildfire to the rest of the world (ongoing even to date). This marks the turn toward the great Industrial Society, Society 3.0.

Mass production of the greatest of the inventions—locomotives and lightbulbs—garner the limelight. Things used to be handcrafted are now mass produced, which will eventually lead to shifting the manufacturing of everything from in-house and mom and pop shops to factories. Machines are created to replace hard manual labor. These machines not only make things easier, they do it faster, and at a scale only matched by a structured supply chain. Technology rapidly develops, creating more efficient factories. Growth in supply brings goods to everyone, raising the demand. Factories create millions of jobs around the world, growing the global economy.

A bulb pops up in the mind of the great American inventor Thomas Alva Edison, and the whole world lights up, conquering the night for the first time. The world starts to grow smaller through inventions in communication technologies. Telephones and telegrams bring people across the globe together. The mighty steam engines huff, followed by more powerful combustion engines, leading to the creation of automobiles, trains, and eventually airplanes. Further developments in science and technology help us further tackle nature's difficulties, including advancements in medical science. We figure out ways to produce and distribute energy. We expand to parts of the world previously unknown. Brand-new industries evolve around specific products and services. And most importantly, the change occurs at such an extremely fast pace that changes in normal play speed look like a fast-forwarded tape.

Think about it. It takes our planet around 4.5 billion years to produce humans. It takes us, the humans, almost just 300,000 years to win over nature for our necessity: food. Compare that to the progress made in just two centuries since the Industrial Revolution.

Society 4.0: The Information Society

Our time machine is doing an excellent job of giving us a tour of our history, slowing down at the right spots and giving us the highlights of our spectacular 4.5-billion-year past. It detects another major change and slows in the 1970s to mark the beginning of yet another society, a society full of computers and information, also known as Society 4.0 (*Encyclopedia of Communication and Information* 2022). Experiments to create computers to process data finally succeed with the invention of circuit-based modern-day computers after multiple attempts through punched card, steam, and vacuum tube-based technologies, among others. The evolution of the Internet gives everyone the access to information, bringing people around the globe closer together.

Information technology percolates deep into the human psyche, their lifestyle, and their industries, thus increasing dependency across all domains. Humans turn to computers to solve complex problems and get the necessary information. Interpersonal communication improves significantly, allowing anyone across the globe to communicate instantly. Computers grow smaller and more powerful. Thanks to cloud computing, big chunks of data are no longer a human hassle.

The Industrial Revolution not only continues into this new information society, it goes to an all-new level. Information technology shapes businesses and drives their fate. Due to their access to information, businesses and individuals make better decisions. Businesses that embrace technology and take advantage of it prosper. The ones that don't, risk annihilation. Big businesses, such as Blockbuster, Kodak, Circuit City, Sears, and numerous others, get demolished due to lack of innovation.

The good is this: the change picks up more speed, compared to the previous industrialized society. Modern techniques pervade faster across all industries. Tech companies become standalone businesses and rank among the top, completely disrupting almost every business in existence. Entirely new tech-focused subindustries emerge across every sector. For example, the fintech industry evolves through companies, such as PayPal, Square, Marcus, and so on, disrupts traditional financial services firms, and redefines banking. Social media firms such as Facebook disrupt traditional media. Entertainment-tech companies such as Netflix disrupt traditional entertainment companies. Auto-tech companies such as Tesla disrupt traditional automakers. Retail-tech companies such as Amazon disrupt traditional retailers. Hospitality-tech companies such as Airbnb disrupt traditional hospitality companies. Travel-tech companies such as Uber redefine traditional taxis and limousine businesses. Food-tech companies such as Doordash transform the food industry. The list goes on.

Finally, it's time that we gave the time machine a much-wanted break to reflect upon what we witnessed. Back to the present day.

While a few societies are still in 3.0 or even 2.0—in some rare cases, in remote parts of the world—4.0 is where most of the world is now. From the automobile industry to warehousing, from small businesses to unicorns, and from Arctica to Antarctica, no business in any industry is immune to this information revolution. The only way forward for any business in any corner of the world is to add technology to the tail end, or risk going out of business.

It's not just businesses. Information technology dominates everyone's day-to-day lives. Need a ride? No more calling a taxi. Order an Uber. Need to go somewhere you don't know? There's a map at your fingertips. Even better, with the emergence of self-driving cars, you could simply tell the car your destination and do nothing. Want to talk to your mom across the ocean? Forget about the long lines outside a telephone booth. Use a messaging app for free. Need to send a message to your friend? Writing and posting letters is history. Simply post it on Facebook. More importantly, a trip to the store is no longer needed. Order things online. Smartphones replace landlines and even televisions. Slowly, any individual without basic technical knowledge becomes irrelevant. We don't need to go very far into the past and bring someone along to see the change. A visit from a decade ago into the present would absolutely blow the minds of anyone, should something like that happen.

Society 5.0: The Next-Generation Society

We are currently going through another major change, one that will be way different from anything we have seen thus far. While computers have evolved greatly in our information society, we turn to one machine for one set of tasks and a different machine for another. Another way to look at it is that humans babysit machines. We are currently entering a brand-new society, Society 5.0—a futuristic society where machines communicate with each other without an intermediary to provide a coordinated end-to-end experience to their human masters. Machines learn over time and become smarter to serve their master the best. Humans are at the center of society, surrounded by these smart, connected machines that enrich life. Whether we like it or not, this is happening, and we must get ready, or else we will face disruption.

So, in this seemingly unpredictable world, can you envisage how the world is going to look like in the future, how we're going to contribute to it, and how we can benefit from it? But first, we must analyze our past to learn from it. We must understand the currents ahead to successfully navigate through them. The purpose of this book is to do exactly that: to equip you with the information you need about the future while taking a glimpse at how we got to today so that you can exploit the future in your own way. This book will help you get a 360-degree view of the future so that you can make a choice—not just any choice but an informed choice—that is right for you in the ocean of future possibilities to make the best use of your skills in a world that waits for none.

CHAPTER 2

Falcon's Tale

A fine Friday morning, April 26, 2047, immediately after the end of the war that had rattled the world for almost a year; all the communication channels were restored; transport systems were reopened; and transactions were reallowed. It was the day of the New Beginning. It was the day of victory for humankind, once again.

There was something unique about the Third World War. Unlike the first two during which the countries strove to overrun each other, this time the most hostile of the enemies banded together to put up a fight against their common enemy, against a machine that had no shape and form, that was nowhere and still everywhere—an artificially intelligent entity.

Though an early riser, Falcon lay deep in bed that day as he was up late witnessing the Operation Peace Chain Live, a peace treaty signed by all the world leaders. Falcon's mom, Pixel, stood unobtrusively at a corner as if without will or compulsion. It was complete mayhem after Pixel had left; Falcon never knew how to deal with the brutal world while losing the only family he had, his mom.

Falcon was an ordinary Joe of the late 21st century. He loved climbing rocks but was a construction worker by profession. Pixel (1968–2037) worked day and night to raise Falcon and Dragon, Falcon's baby brother, also a construction worker. Building was at the heart of Falcon's and Dragon's life, given their living was built on it from their great ancestors' time. Their ancestors were the original builders during the Dutch tulip mania back in the 1600s. However, as the construction techniques evolved, Falcon and Dragon worked as high-efficiency robotic operators (HERO) in the field.

Pixel had to be put in an induced coma from the beginning of the war, from which she came back earlier this morning. She rushed toward Falcon despite her frailty and whispered with all her lungs could force.

"Son, wake up," she said. "I'm back."

Falcon woke up with one big thrust and jumped off the bed. Astounded, he ran to his mom and gave her a tight hug.

"When? Mom, how long have you been here?" Falcon said, his eyes dampened. "I missed you."

The raising curtains made way to the first light of that morning. Kneeled at the floor, Falcon looked incessantly at his mother's lit face.

"The light of freedom feels great," said Falcon, looking outside the window.

"We're in this together now, son."

Not wanting to miss this moment, Falcon blinked his eyes thrice to take a picture.

Pixel rushed toward the kitchen. She seemed absolutely fine.

"Drink this. I think we ran out of your favorite one. I brewed some Calinga for now and ordered a pack of Kona. It's on the drone already and will be here at 8.03. I will brew another one once it's here." Falcon looked at his coffee with utter curiosity.

"We don't have Kona? Shouldn't Ruby order one by now?"

"No, she's broken. They analyzed the data; there was an error during the update. It'll be fixed."

"They have to send someone. What's going on?" said Falcon.

"It seems the sensor needs to be replaced. They don't have an ETA yet…they're overwhelmed because of the war," Pixel sighed.

Ruby is their pantry.

"Finish your morning run and go, get ready. Gamze already has your clothes ready." Gamze is their closet.

Falcon blinked his eyes multiple times to turn on the jog mode in his head. After 27 minutes, his T-shirt warned him that it's time to slow down and head to the shower.

He finished his shower, got ready, and sat for breakfast. He could smell his favorite coffee. "Delivered in 7 minutes. Not bad."

He gradually raised his nose around the coffee cup and breathed in the vapor. He reached the breakfast table. Something was strange.

There were two sets of plates. He knew that his mom doesn't eat.

"Mom, who're these for?"

"For Pascal, sweetheart. Is she not joining us?"

Getting a plate ready for Pascal, Falcon's wife, would be deemed normal for Pixel. But Pascal had been dead for a little over two years.

"Mom, are you okay? I think you should rest for a while."

"Oh," Pixel said and immediately removed the plate. "Sorry. I miss her so much I sometimes forget she's not here."

Falcon loved his wife, and he misses her. Memories abound.

He took a long breath.

Pixel pretends that she forgets. She has no memories of the clothes Falcon wears, of the accident that took Pascal away, or that Pascal wasn't around to eat together.

Falcon realized that something didn't add up. His mom was in a coma for a year, but these were memories from the prior years.

"You remember nothing?"

She started to recollect. Nothing came back. A year and a half before? Nothing. Two years? None. She figured she didn't remember anything that happened in the last three years.

Pixel connected with her twin Zyxel. All files were untampered and intact except that of May 13, 2044. It was gone.

"That's horrible. What happened? Did someone tamper with them?" she wondered. "How is Falcon going to react to this news? Should I even tell him?"

She decided to keep it to herself.

Pixel recollected some of Falcon's childhood memories and slowly took the conversation to Pascal, then their wedding, and all the good times they had together. The idea was to get Falcon to talk about the past three years, so Pixel could register that in memory and pretend that she's not completely lost on this.

"I should have listened to you. That day…you warned us not to…I wish I'd never taken her to that rock climbing trip."

"Yeah…I mean no, you don't have to feel sorry, no. But you can talk about it now."

"That was like hell. I lost my legs but I umm…had enough savings and I got new legs. You see these? And here… spine fixed, eyes… vision restored. Like that. But I wish I had those wings as well like Rocco."

That was a lot to learn for Pixel. She created transient slots and fitted all that Falcon said in her memory.

"How do you feel now? Any tingling on your feet?"

"No, they're magnificent, yeah. I feel normal now," replied Falcon. "It takes two years—that's what the doc said and now it's been two years."

Falcon slowly went down the memory lane and started recollecting everything that had occurred since the accident. How he underwent all those surgeries and what it was like during the accident—he recollected them all. He's been saving money to bring Pascal back one day—spotting that Pixel understood and registered it all. Pixel wanted Falcon to give away everything that might reinstate her memory.

"The war…it was devastating. This set my savings for Pascal back by a year," continued Falcon.

Now that Pixel figured out what happened to Falcon and Pascal, and when it happened, she quickly figured the series of care Falcon needs to go through. She gained access to his medical records. He was due for a spine adjustment. She connected with the doctor's office and made an appointment.

"You are due for your spine adjustment, son. I set up an appointment with Dr. Birx for 10.45. Go, get it done before you travel for work. By the way, you have been assigned to a Scottish castle. I just accessed the plan and the schedule. Do you know there will be a Taj Mahal next door? I bet the view will be awesome once it's all built."

Meantime, little Snowflake brought Falcon's shoes.

"Snowflake. I forgot about you buddy. Great to see you," Falcon yelled.

Little Snowflake is tiny but sturdy, with fleshy metallic arms and moving parts. He is their little helper at home. A smart one. Snowflake had to be put in a coma during the war as well. Well, not a medically induced coma, but a digital one, like Pixel had.

"Hey, I've got Electron for you. She's waiting outside," said little Snowflake. Electron is Falcon's car.

"It was on charge. I turned it off earlier this morning because the bricks were low on power. It has enough juice to get you to the nearest charging road, though," Snowflake continued.

"Thanks, flaky. Catch you later."

"Slow down Romeo, you're still in bad shape." Snowflake is always worried about Falcon. But he doesn't like being called flaky.

Falcon walked toward Electron who was waiting with the door open. "Good to go?"

He nodded. She switched on the gravosuspension and projected Falcon's body vitals in the air.

"It's a beautiful day today, isn't it?" Electron struck a conversation. "Aren't you glad the war is over?"

"Tell me about it. I am breathing the freedom."

Electron sensed Falcon's damp forehead and scrolled the window down.

"By the way, we are 16 percent charged right now. We will be full by the time we reach the doctor's office. It will be 1.6 coins," said Electron.

"I wish I got enough money one day to join that Walker Club," said Falcon, looking at a group of folks walking outside. "I am tired of getting my exercise within the four walls of the house, you know."

"The membership to that club is 100 coins a month. You can cut your coffee intake to one cup every other day, which will save you nine coins. You can reduce my use to less than 6 hours a week, which will allow me to generate additional 39 coins for you. You will still be short unless you get a pay hike."

"I know. Walking is only for those privileged," said Falcon as he responded to a beep on his wrist.

"Yeah, it is. We are approaching the Sacramento Airway."

They came to a stop, got on to the elevator together, and entered the Sacramento, San Francisco 3D Airway in seconds.

"3, 2, 1, take off," a low voice narrated.

There they are, traveling at 300 miles per hour. A beam of light flashed on their faces at regular intervals. They reached the ground floor.

"Total time: 14 minutes. Thank you for using our service. Have a good day."

Electron took over and drove Falcon to the doctor's office in San Francisco. As soon as they reached the doctor's office, they were greeted by Cortana, the invisible front office manager.

"Welcome, Mr. Falcon. How are you doing today?" Cortana said. "How has your spine been?"

"Not much troubling."

"You know the drill, but I need to repeat this for you. You are on camera. We use your information only for medical purpose. Please smile if you accept."

Falcon gave a big bright smile.

"You are a few minutes early. Would you like to go to the restroom? Better have the urine assay ready before the doctor arrives."

"Well. It's time to go see the talking toilet," said Falcon, smirking.

"Sure. I activated the access door for you," Cortana said.

Falcon moved in. He stood in front of a urine-pod and let it through in the pod's stopper-like graphite block.

"Analyzing the sample…," it said.

"Okay doctor toilet." Falcon raised his eyebrows in distaste.

"Color: Yellow. Appearance: Clear. Specific gravity: 1.02. RBC: Nil. Pus cells: 0–1. Cast: …"

"Synchronizing the results…Report synchronized. Thank you," the voice said.

Falcon went back to the doctor's room.

"Dr. Birx is waiting for you, Mr. Falcon," Cortana said.

Falcon proceeded. Dr. Birx sat in a climate-controlled chair in his office.

"Hello, Mr. Falcon. How are you today? Aren't you glad the war is finally over?" the doctor said.

"Hi, Dr. Birx. Good to see you. Yes, indeed. It was the longest and darkest…"

"It was worse than COVID back then. By the way, it looks like you are doing great. All your reports came out fine. Your spine and leg alignments look excellent. I can see that your walking has improved. Your sitting posture is good. Umm…Your spine is excellent. I double-checked all the reports myself, and yes…your urine output is improving: they look fantastic. You just need this final adjustment. Jes will be in shortly for it."

Jes is Dr. Birx's physiotherapy assistant bot. Falcon took off his shoes and lay down on the table. Jes came in shortly and finished the adjustment.

"You're all set, Mr. Falcon. Cortana will inform you of the steps ahead," said Jes.

Falcon wore his shoes, adjusted his clothes, and walked out of the room.

"Looks like you had a good visit today, Mr. Falcon."

"Yes, indeed Cort. It was excellent. Thanks. When's my next visit due, by the way?"

"With your adjustments done, we need to monitor you for a year. You have two options. You can come in every month, or we can do this remotely through Pixel or Snowflake. What do you prefer?"

"Can we do a hybrid? You can work it out with Snowflake, but I'll be back in six months."

"Just a second. Let me make sure I am friends with Snowflake. Can you please confirm that Snowflake's ID is H78K6F? Also need your permission to connect with Snowflake."

"That's right." Falcon gave a big smile to confirm the connection with Snowflake.

"Do you want full or partial remote monitoring? Full monitoring will be 89.4 coins cheaper than the partial. Snowflake just recommended full."

"I'll go for full, especially if Snowflake approved the financials behind it. That's convenient," answered Falcon, smiling.

"Thank you, Mr. Falcon. I know we delivered your pills manually for the past year. We are back to business as usual, and I just sent your pill details to Zayan, as instructed by Snowflake. I will also work with Snowflake to set up the next appointment as we get closer to the six-month mark. And of course, we will contact you before that if we find anything out of the ordinary."

Zayan is Falcon's 3D printer.

"Sure. That's great." Falcon said, "By the way, how much did today's visit cost me? Will it be drawn today?"

"None, Mr. Falcon. Today's visit has been paid for by your health coins."

"Oh! That's excellent. Am I not glad I'm participating in the health coin program?"

"Yes, Mr. Falcon. Everyone feels the same. Anyway, have a good day."

"Bye."

Falcon walked out of the doctor's office. Electron was already waiting for him at the front door.

"Are we going back home?" she asked.

"Can't wait. My stomach's rumbling."

"We will reach home at 11.59. Lunch will be ready by then. Pixel confirmed," said Electron.

"Excellent. By the way, I wonder how Dragon is doing. I haven't heard from him yet. I know they were supposed to turn on all the communications by now."

Electron tried to check if the communication channels for Dragon are open. Meantime, Falcon received a call from his brother.

"Never mind. He just contacted me."

"Hey." Falcon got busy "talking" to his baby brother with his eyes closed while Electron drove him home.

"Talking has changed so much lately, isn't it? People used to 'speak' through phones before. It's all telepathic now," said Electron, striking a conversation once Falcon finished speaking to his brother.

"Yes, indeed. It took me a while to get used to it, but I cannot imagine using a phone any longer."

They were home. It was 11.59 as Electron's dashboard reminded.

Falcon could smell the fresh aroma of basil. Pixel set up the table for one person this time.

***

Let's pause the story for a while and analyze what happened thus far.

The story of Falcon's life will be the story of your life, my life, and everyone's life one day, as the technology becomes more advanced every day. Falcon will live the rest of his life, no doubt, and perhaps he will bring his wife back one day. But I'm sure we have a lot of questions to answer.

There seems to be a thin line between humans and machines. Snowflake, Electron, and Cortana behave like humans. How did they become intelligent? Machines and people seem to communicate directly. How did that work? More, there's a lot of mind-reading going on in the story. Was it mind-reading or something else? How was that done? Was Pixel alive? Did she have a cousin? What is a jog mode in the head? How did Electron charge while driving? What is the story with payment in coins? Was it bitcoin? What is a 3D airway? How was Falcon able to agree to the terms and conditions with a smile? How was Cortana planning to monitor Falcon through Snowflake? Sending pill details to a printer? How did that urine test work? Above all, what is the story of the Scottish castle with a Taj Mahal view? We will dig into the answers to these questions in the following chapters.

CHAPTER 3

The BIG Highlights

After a failed flight attempt, Wilbur Wright frustratingly said to his brother Orville, "Not within a thousand years would man ever fly" (Wright-brothers n.d.). That was the prediction of 1901. And that was how impossible flying was then, also discouraging. In 1903, however, Orville and Wilbur Wright built the first flying machine. And the rest is history as we know it today.

Napoleon said in the early 1800s: "What, sir, would you make a ship sail against the wind and currents by lighting a bonfire under her deck? I pray you excuse me, I have no time to listen to such nonsense" (Holley 1997). The first successful steamboat was the Clermont, which was built by American inventor Robert Fulton in 1807.

Whales will be domesticated and used for transportation. Rail tracks will be built at the edge of water and boats will sail right onto these and move on the ground. The horse is here to stay but the automobile is only a novelty. Electricity is just a fad. There are hundreds of predictions that proved to be true, can't count, that prove the clairvoyance of our esteemed ancestors. But at the same time, there were also predictions that went wrong. Dead wrong.

We will slowly but surely dissect Falcon's life story, the one you read in the beginning. While we will take a deeper look into the future, I want to cover the highlights first. But there are a few important things to consider before we start. First, let me clarify I'm not passing judgments here to say things out of the blue. Informed prediction is different from guesses and far different from clairvoyance in terms of "dismissibility." Second, predicting the future is difficult. We consider a lot of factors, not just limited to what is technically possible, but also what is socially and politically feasible, among other things. One way to predict the future is to analyze the past trends and extrapolate them into the best possible scenario which is what I try to do here. Thus, the historical context acts as a good launching pad into the future. Third, future predictions are often based on what is available at the time. It's difficult to predict what will be invented in the future. For example, Wilbur Wright didn't know that he, along with his brother, would invent an airplane because no artificial thing could fly then. This means we take what is available today and build on that to predict the future. This book will make certain predictions backed by today's emerging science and technologies; however, I might also make some speculations, which I will call out.

Your T-Shirt Will Talk to You

Look around and describe the things around you. In fact, let me describe to you what I see. One-way communication here is easier than waiting for your answers in my e-mail later. I see a laptop, a cell phone, a refrigerator, a stove, a coffee maker, an oven, a dishwasher, a few chairs, a dining table, a thermostat, a few lights, a pantry, a microwave, a mirror, and a few other things. I am sure you are surrounded by something similar. Now, look at what you are wearing. I am wearing pants, a t-shirt, and a Fitbit.

What does this have to do with artificial intelligence (AI)? Mainly, what does "the BIG future" have to do with how you are dressed now? All inventions, whether daily use or specialized, will have one thing in common in the future: AI. Some of them already have some AI built in; the rest will get their AI sometime in the future.

Last time you shopped online, did you notice the recommendations on what to buy next? Who do you think is sending you those recommendations? These smart marketing gimmicks are called upselling and cross-selling and are powered by AI. An algorithm analyzes your interests through past purchases and your purchase patterns and shows what you may be interested in. Like online retailers, your daily social feeds are also sent to you by AI catering to your interests and usage history. If you use Google maps, *they* are powered by AI. AI powers ridesharing apps like Uber. From cars to airplanes, AI is dominating the way machines work and, ultimately, humans.

Machines, such as ovens and microwaves, incorporating AI are common. But a smart chair? Smart clothes? People have enough ideas already to instill "intelligence" in these devices. Some car seats are already smart to self-heat themselves and adjust them to the comfort of the driver. They will only get smarter.

Today, mirrors cannot just talk to you; they also teach you important health tips. The company Lululemon has unveiled a smart mirror which projects a human trainer on the person's mirror and offers smart training sessions live (Suarez 2022). They're only blooming buds, however. Clothes are already getting smart and developing into wearables. We can expect them to be more sophisticated in the coming days. The smart clothes industry is blooming rapidly and is expected to be a $5.3 billion business by 2024, according to markets-and-markets.com (Marketsand-markets 2022).

Imagine you're on your way to work and you hear a notification from your t-shirt: *High body temperature detected. Take a day off from work.* That's around the corner. Bad news to couch potatoes—your sofa or couch will ask you to take a walk because you have been sitting for too long. Your door will lock itself if you forget. Windows (your house's), tables, pantries, fans, appliances, switches, light bulbs, frames, accessories— they are gaining intelligence turning your home smarter.

Talking of smart homes, one of the most intelligent human smart-home inventions is in the toilet. A smart toilet or technically a pan or commode is a poop-changing concept I am personally fascinated with, and I don't think people are taking their poop-bins seriously. Self-flushing or cleaning toilets are not a big deal these days; I'm not referring to them. A smart toilet that analyzes your waste and detects diseases at their early stage would be the ultimate game. For instance, you have COVID but are you asymptomatic? You have a pathology-enabled toilet that can tell you that. I hate to say this, but the most important health diagnoses may not happen in a diagnosis center but in your toilet. Fecal immunochemical tests (FIT) can diagnose colorectal cancer at its early stage (Amitay et al. 2019). The only downside—each time you go to poop, your family members may eagerly wait outside for the results.

So, not very far in the future, AI will be everywhere. There is no doubt AI will dominate our life completely. There's no denying that something that's employed on a day-to-day basis from social media applications to self-driving cars will change the way we live, work, and eat. Unless you live in a cave somewhere, you are a beneficiary of AI day in, day out.

Well, maybe I should call you a user instead of a beneficiary—that's the "proper" industry term.

Smart Gets Smarter Over Time

Smart switches, smart doors, smart thermostats, smart stoves, smart garage door openers, smart light bulbs, smart vacuum cleaners, smart washing machines. Smart things here, smart things there, smart things everywhere—even on Mars and outside the solar system. We already live in a smart universe. Today's world is filled with a myriad of such smart things. Now what do I mean when I say AI will dominate our life? Do I mean they will simply continue to grow more in number?

The word "smart" will be more literal with time, making decisions for us without our intervention. A switch will not be called a smart switch only because it can be controlled remotely from a smartphone. A garage door opener will not be called smart just because it is connected to a smartphone and can be operated from anywhere. The same applies to any future smart things.

Futuristic smart things must be able to learn over time and become smarter through a method commonly referred to as machine learning. A part of AI, machine learning enables machines (things) to learn from their data over time to get smarter and provide an experience of companionship to its masters. For example, a futuristic smart electric switch learns from your past usage pattern and, over time, can turn itself off based on your past behavior. A smart thermostat will learn all your preferences over time and automatically adjust the temperature to your liking, based on the time of the day and your activities. A smart door will automatically know when you are not home and lock itself.

To sum up, everything around you will turn into smart helpers with one and only one goal: to serve their master, that is, you. They will do so not just by being available to you, but also by learning about you to provide that personalized experience.

Smart Is Not Enough; Sharing Is the Key

The term "smart" originates in the information society, Society 4.0. As we saw earlier, smart things will grow not only in number, but also in "brain." However, it doesn't stop there. Smart things will connect more people all over the world. But the true smartness lies in their ability to connect nonliving and living things together, mostly everyday things. These interconnected things that can talk with each other over a network are called the Internet of Things (IoT).

An IoT garage door can talk to your car, "ask" it to open it on your arrival or exit. What if your garage door can check with the car when it's left open and close itself? What if your main door can talk to your car or the garage door and lock itself if you forgot, based on the response from your car or the garage door? What if your car or the thermostat can tell itself to turn off when you are away? What if your refrigerator and pantry coordinate to prepare a grocery list automatically placed by your digital assistant and delivered home? What if other smart things such as washing machine and printer join this team to collectively prepare the list? While we are at it, why not add smart bulbs and smart batteries to join this team to add themselves to the list when they go bad? The idea is these smart things talk to each other to provide an integrated and automated experience to you.

These coordinated experiences will not be limited to your home. Talking objects will traverse the land, fly in the air, swim inside water, and dwell underground. On the road, your digital assistant may read your calendar and book a vehicle beforehand thus passing on your preferences. The ride arrives—temperature adjusted to your preference—and the driver turns off the music and keeps a quiet environment for you because he knows you like silence while travelling.

Imagine your thermostat following you around the world when you travel. Not literally, but digitally. Whenever you enter a prebooked hotel room, you will certainly have that "feels-like-home" experience as your room's thermostat passes on your preferences to the hotel room' thermostat.

In short, future machines will not only learn over time, but also coordinate with other machines constantly to provide you with an end-to-end experience.

You May Be Sitting on a Goldmine

I was searching for AI consultants on Google, and the next thing I knew, I had recommendations on Facebook for the same. A post about travel accessories looks interesting to you; you click on it now. The next moment you get advertisements related to these accessories. Such personalized shopping experiences through targeted advertisement are becoming more common these days.

Information technology has existed for over a few decades, but we surely are at an inflection point, with AI growing its footprint rapidly. What is different now compared to a decade ago? How are these AI-bots able to know your preferences so accurately they know you better than you know yourself? The answer is the "I" in the IT, that is, information.

AI can now process the vast number of digital crumbs you leave behind every moment through your actions on the Internet, thanks to technologies like "big data," thus creating your digital profile. Your digital-existential CV, so to say. The more crumbs you leave, the more information it gathers about you. Knowledge makes you smarter. The more knowledge you gain, the smarter you become. What makes the AI smarter? The answer is the same—knowledge. The other way to say it is "information" also known as data.

Your data are your gold mine. Each day you surf the Internet, AI tracks your data for free, collects your information like a vacuum cleaner sucking dust. Indeed, you have the option not to share your data. And to any rational citizen, sharing limited data in exchange for the "service" the platform offers seems a fair deal.

But is that enough of a reward? Imagine getting a kickback from the advertisement money your e-commerce company earns in exchange for your information it shares with the product seller. It's not unreasonable to expect it. The more data you share, the more money you make—isn't this a better business model? This can be a great way to make money from the comfort of your couch, doing things you normally do. I strongly believe we will get there soon.

But there is more.

Let's say you are hitting your bed early, with hours of sleep, eating a healthy diet, and exercising every day. You share these data with your health insurance company. Because you're adopting such a healthy lifestyle, your health insurance company will send you a bonus check. Do not, however, take that as a favor. You get rewarded because you are keeping yourself fit and doing everything to reduce the risk of catching a disease.

But how does your health insurance company know all of these? Through your wearable devices that track your activity and digital assistant placing your grocery orders. But what if I shop in store? Even if you shop in store, your grocery store, in future, might track your purchases through facial recognition and share that with the health care company. Again, all of this will happen only if you consent to the sharing. But, given the monetary rewards, why wouldn't you want to share your data?

The possibilities are endless. For example, your smart car can share your driving history with your insurance company. You will get a bonus check before you know it. You let your social media company sell your information to a research firm or a political organization. You get a share of that money. You let Maps track your history, come up with patterns, and share them with businesses around the places you visit. You take a certain route every day. Map applications share your information with businesses on the way to offer you discounts. You get a share of the money your map is getting. This list can go on.

While each transaction may get you only a little, the cumulative amount will become a significant chunk. Will this lay the path for future universal basic income?

The Big Boss Will Have the Smartest AI

Silicon Valley has the best talent in the world and attracts global investments. After all, it's the tech-capital of the United States and probably the smartest place on earth.

Before you go down that compelling argument, let me tell you: *China* will be the smartest country in the world.

Let me clarify before things get political here. China is headed to become the smartest country not because it will create the best technology. It is also not because it will bear the smartest people on earth or build the best infrastructures. That may or may not be the case, but that's not the reason.

It's because of its data. The more data AI has, the smarter it becomes. We can confidently say Chinese AI will have the richest data compared to any country in the world. Partly, it is due to their huge population. More people generate more data, and more training data means more "intelligent" AI. However, the main reason is the type of data on top of the number. Privacy laws are easier to make in the one-party Chinese government with low chances of decent. Chinese government can obtain the data from all their citizens, an entirely different story in case of a democratic country, such as the United States, where people's privacy is not only respected, but also protected by law.

In July 2018, the *New York Times* reported that a Chinese police officer in a train station in Zhengzhou city spotted a heroin smuggler using facial recognition sunglasses. "In Qingdao," wrote the *Times* ahead, "cameras powered by artificial intelligence helped the police snatch two dozen criminal suspects in the midst of a big annual beer festival" (Mozur 2018). The article was titled "Inside China's Dystopian Dreams: AI, Shame and Lots of Cameras."

China is embracing technologies, such as facial recognition and AI, to identify and track its 1.4 billion people with a goal to minimize crimes. Most of the tracking is done through the security cameras placed all over the city. Facial recognition is used to prevent even the pettiest of the crimes, jay walking, for example. A picture and the name of the person in violation are displayed on the street for public shaming. Fines are automatically sent to the address on the file. There are massive dashboards in the central government location to monitor these activities. We have also seen reports of how China has used technology to keep people at home during the COVID-19 pandemic (Kharpal 2020). That level of surveillance is simply unimaginable in most other countries, especially the United States.

The Ticket to the Sky

For thousands of years, humans have walked on land to go from one place to another. We invented a wheel that moved us faster, figured ways to use animals for transport, and invented wheel carts. After James Watt improved Thomas Newcomen's steam engine (Rolt and Allen 1977) and made it efficient, long- and heavy-load-bearing transportation became a reality. Then, the industrial era exploded when eventually a combustion engine made the land transportation faster and better. Meanwhile, we figured out a way to travel for a long time on water as well, using manual boats and ships to eventually turn them into engine-run beasts with the mightiest of the bodies.

Thanks to Wright brothers' 20th-century invention, people could travel in the air too—the fastest form of transportation thus far. Today, we can travel from one corner of the world to another in a day without feeling like traveling, and flying is now touted as the safest form of transportation ever invented. Could we imagine this prior to the invention of an airplane? Traveling across oceans used to take months.

This is all about to get better. As of 2022, a new dimension is taking shape in the transportation realm, in addition to land, water, and air—the space.

In a matter of few years, you will be able to travel from Bali to Raleigh or North Pole to South Pole in less than an hour. Traveling from one corner of the earth to another in hours, not days, will no longer be a surprise. Imagine getting your breakfast at home, attending a meeting entirely on a different side of the world, and being back home for lunch. That day is coming soon, all thanks to advancements in space travel. Here is how.

Elon Musk declared in 2017 that his company Space X will build rocket-powered vehicles that're expected to be tested soon, which will enable intercity travel in a matter of minutes (Wall 2022). You might go to a "spaceport" where you will board a spaceship or a space bus, similar to an airbus, but launch yourself to the space rather than just the air. Once you reach space, the lack of air resistance will make you travel at speeds of up to 17,500 miles per hour (Jones 2017). When you reach your destination in space, you re-enter the atmosphere and reach the spaceport. As crazy as it sounds, this form of transportation is not very far in time. Buckle up and get ready because future travel will be superfast.

Flying Cars May Never Fly

This may come as a surprise to some. Flying cars have been a thematic part in several science fiction movies, a concept thrown around for decades. But sadly, flying cars may never hit our roads on a commercial level.

In fact, flying cars have been in our airway for a while now. They are called helicopters. Not just cars, flying buses have also been carrying hundreds of passengers at a time; they are called airplanes. Long-distance transport vehicles with dedicated places to take off and land are practical and easy to make, at least today. The challenge is making a vehicle that can land on any land as well as fly in air.

The flying car driver is now a pilot-driver and needs to have a flying license and an extensive training on both. What if we make the ones hitting the lower skies electric and self-driving to work around the pilot training requirement? You can call it a car-drone. It may cost a fortune today to buy one; only mass production, driven by massive demand, may eventually reduce the costs.

The battery technology needs significant improvement to cover a decent amount of distance to make it practical. The best prototype model today flies for under 30 minutes without having to land for a recharge. That's a nonstarter, given they need around 30 minutes of reserve power just in case of landing delays. However, extensive research on energy storage/battery technologies may ultimately fruit, producing lighter but higher energy batteries.

However, tougher challenges will hit after we cross the first set of barriers. Imagine your life with a bunch of cars or drones flying around. How would you feel? At what height will these cars fly? Who will own the air space? We certainly don't want any foreign objects on the top of our houses, especially those with a flat roof you can walk on. What control do homeowners have? Meaning, how much of the air space above the house is owned by the homeowners? Most importantly, how do we regulate massive amounts of traffic in the air when regulating well-organized roads? Do I see practical use cases for flying cars? Yes, ambulances, for example. Airlifting patients is a common practice in several parts of the world today. However, let's just call them helicopters and not confuse them with flying cars.

But what about the flying taxi the media has been filled with lately? Dubai has tested an autonomous air taxi (AAT) that can fly up to two people at a time over a short distance. While the challenges I outlined earlier also apply to them, these are not meant to be flying cars; instead, they call them flying taxis. The best way to understand them is to call them autonomous helicopters or passenger drones.

No More Traffic Jams

One thing we all hate is traffic jam. Not sure about you, but I haven't met a person who loves traffic jams, unless he is facing his boss' wrath the following day.

"Beating traffic jams" next to "flying cars are not possible" might sound contradictory. But flying cars won't be the solution to traffic jams despite the number of vehicles and people being added to the streets. If not them, then what?

Two major revolutions will contribute the most to this multifold question's answer. The first is autonomous vehicle revolution. I think it's safe to say that future roads will be filled with autonomous vehicles—not just cars, but vans, trucks, and buses. The day human driving is not allowed in the major super/highways is around the corner. It may not happen within a decade or so because it will take a while for the regulations and infrastructure to forge, but it will happen eventually.

What are the best features of autonomous cars? They are best drivers, most certainly better than average humans, especially in a well-controlled environment filled with other autonomous vehicles. Most accidents are the products of human errors. When we take humans out of the driving equation altogether, think about how safe our roadways will become. For example, look at how safe airplanes are in their auto-pilot mode. But other than being safe, autonomous cars will follow a structured approach to driving, making traffic jams less likely.

However, autonomous cars will not eliminate traffic jams completely. There will still be congestion on our roadways, especially during peak hours. There will still be traffic lights, causing delays and alleviating jams, especially around cities. How do we overcome this problem? This is where the second revolution comes in—what I call the Boring Revolution, owing to Elon Musk.

Instead of flying in the air, The Boring Company is working on flying under the ground using a technology they call "The Loop" (Park 2022). This technology will eventually turn traveling a truly 3D experience, enabling flying under the ground. But what does it even mean to fly under the ground? The concept is pretty simple (yet difficult to implement). Areas experiencing heavy traffic jams can take the underground route and bypass the excess. This concept is no different than the tunnels we have been digging for decades now. The devil is in the details.

The Boring Company describes the Loop as "an all-electric, zero-emissions, high-speed underground public transportation system in which passengers are transported via compatible Autonomous Electric Vehicles (AEVs) at up to 150 miles per hour through Main Artery Tunnels between stations" (The Boring Company 2022). The Loop is projecting speeds of up to 150 miles per hour, for example (Cheng 2018). They have bored a tunnel to travel from Las Vegas Convention Center to Mandalay Bay in 3 minutes, which usually takes 30 minutes ("Projects" 2023).

These 3D tunnels are smaller in diameter compared to traditional tunnels that are easier to dig. The smaller diameter is to do with how these tunnels operate. Traditional tunnels work the same way as open roads. We drive our car into the tunnel and out of it on a lane. On the contrary, 3D tunnels will be autonomous. Multiple options are being considered to make them efficient. One option for the Loop is to use a self-driving car's tires. However, several variations of this have been discussed that work for nonautonomous cars as well. In one variation of this model that could apply to any vehicle, once the car reaches the tunnel, it will enter a small elevator that takes it inside the tunnel. Similar to suitcases put in small bins in airports while passing through the security or toward the baggage claim, the car becomes the suitcase and the bin, a giant moving "bin" inside the tunnel, which moves it to the other side. The car is not driving at all. It is being carried in a bin at a high speed. Another elevator brings the car back to the ground, at which point the car's pilot system takes over. Regardless of specifics, underground flying is the future for sure.

A faster mass transportation version of it called the Hyperloop estimates speeds of up to 760 miles per hour (Huang 2021), the speed of an airplane, operating in a vacuum-sealed tunnel. Hyperloop is more sophisticated than the Loop and will carry passengers faster and farther than it. With speeds like this, do you still need flying cars? The other way to look at this is: *these* will be the underground flying cars.

One Charge Will Take You 1,000 Miles

Electric vehicles (EVs) are the latest add-ons in the automobile world. Smart cars, self-driving cars, autonomous driving cars, moving robots, green cars, clean-energy cars: whatever you call them, they're dominating the streets and for the better. While smartness has nothing to do with the type of fuel used, such as electricity, all of today's futuristic smart cars run with electricity. Smart or not, self-driving or not, it's clear the future of cars is electric.

In August 2021, NBC News wrote: "Biden signs order aiming for half of new vehicles to be electric by 2030. Automakers' expected quick transition from gas-burning cars and trucks to electric is a key part of the White House strategy to fight global warming" (Lederman 2021). In addition to scientists pushing the technology, there are also several governments formulating plans and policies to adopt clean energy transportation in the coming years.

Cars can easily be manufactured to run with electricity. In fact, replacing old-fashioned combustion engines with electric moving parts is not difficult. We have been building electric cars for ages, of course the miniature ones: kids' toys. My point is: at least we have the technology. The dominant name in electric cars is none other than Tesla, which can run from 0 to 60 miles per hour in just 1.99 seconds, insanely fast (Lambert 2021).

The more powerful the engine, the easier the build. What is the issue then? The biggest electric car challenge is power storage. The lithium-ion battery technology we use today is from the 1990s and has two major issues apart from safety, which car manufacturers have figured out how to handle. It takes a long time to charge, but discharges the power fast, making your long-distance travel less than ideal. If you take Model X Plaid as an example, it takes around 45 minutes (as of October 2022) for a full charge on a super charger and gives around 348 miles of range. This is a bigger car and I know there are other models that provide a better range, but not significantly more.

Well, this is all going to change in the future. As I mentioned, the battery technology we use today is old. There has been a battery revolution lately, giving rise to several alternatives to lithium-ion technology.

One interesting technology I want to introduce here is the solid-state battery technology. Solid-state batteries provide very long ranges on one single charge as well as support fast charging. The two fundamental EV challenges are currently expected to be addressed by this technology. Toyota is presently leading the charge in this area with over 1,000 patents (Toyota IE 2022).

In fact, Toyota is only claiming 700-km range on their solid-state batteries that could be charged in less than 15 minutes (*ibid*). Solid-state battery has the potential to provide ranges up to multiple hundreds of miles on a single charge. But this is only one of the many battery technologies under development. Also, it's certain we will have some major breakthroughs soon because of the investment pouring into this area. Many players are in a race to create revolutionary battery technologies, including a ton of startups. This laser and major focus is what gives me the confidence that we will soon build much better batteries.

In case you're wondering why all these advances to this technology are happening now, the answer is: because such magnitude of power was unnecessary. Batteries best serve to power portable devices such as laptops and flashlights. The need for electricity storage is growing like never before owing to the growing innovation in electric vehicles and a constant push toward renewable energy in general. The biggest challenge your utilities company faces is matching the demand for electricity and the supply. They operate as "just-in-time" manufacturing companies of electricity because current electricity storage options are not very practical. What will solve that problem? A better electricity storage or battery technology.

Speaking Machines

Computers only understand zeroes and ones. How do we tell it to do something? Engineers created a text-based interface to interact with computers. In the early days, they had to type commands for every interaction with the computer. For example, moving a file from one location to another needed a command like "MOVE [/Y | /-Y] [drive:][path]file name1[,...]." Imagine writing such commands to every operation you perform daily.

Then came along the graphical user interface (GUI), originally created for commercial use by Steve Jobs, founder of Apple, and reimagined by Bill Gates, founder of Microsoft, that changed the computing world. These gentlemen created a user-friendly abstract layer for the complex workings of the computers to make computer interactions fun and faster.

It became not only easier to interact with computers this way, but also much faster, which opened up a new world of possibilities on what could be done with and through computers. Take any daily operation you perform—browsing, being on social media, playing video games, or simply typing. Either of these tasks would have been painfully difficult or impossible.

Although this GUI of the 1980s and 1990s went through a significant upgrade since then, we still depend heavily on GUI to date. Indeed, smartphones brought in touchscreens. The fingers and the stylus pens became the keys and the cursors. Technologies that let developers build applications to interact more easily with laptops, smartphones, and tablets emerged, although, fundamentally, these are variations of GUI as the base four decades is a long time for any technology to survive in today's world, and we are due for a huge revolution that brings more comfortable computer-interfacing technology to compliment the long-standing GUI.

Then came along speech-to-text technology, which took a turn in the right direction, allowing us to interact with computers through voice commands instead of having to type or using the mouse. We have seen this technology evolve in the last decade or so.

Alexa, remind me to turn on the pool heat at 4.30 pm. Siri, what's the weather today? Tesla, take me to the nearest shopping mall. We can now perform such operations hands-free with personal assistants and car computers. We can also dictate our thoughts on Microsoft word and other programs. When was the last time you used the type function for search on your Apple TV, Roku, or the Fire TV? Talking has become the new word for doing and can save a lot of time, which will only grow in the future.

This technology when enhanced to a certain level will benefit billions of people and potentially save a lot of lives. A field worker working on a hazardous electricity line or a factory worker working with perilous machinery can speak to machines without the hassles of checking it in a device.

Is voice assistance perfect today? Not by any means. At certain times, it's a sophisticated listener, while at other times, it's a toddler. Dictating a full paragraph, even worse, the entire book, does come with challenges. Other challenges include a heavy accent and background noise. However, with machine learning and other advanced AI, speech recognition will be more refined and clever. It won't be long before we get to a point where talking to computers will become the primary mode of human–computer interactions. You can even argue with them if you feel like it. The day is near when graphical interface would be limited to viewing and noise-free operations.

Bad Day for Typing and Speaking

A text-based interface is better than manipulating numbers on a computer. And graphics-based interface is better than writing those complex commands. Likewise, touchscreen-based graphics are better than keyboard and mouse-based operations. A speech-based interface is faster than a graphics-based interface. However, all these interfaces are doing one thing. They are converting the thoughts from our brain into commands the computer can understand. What if we can cut these intermediaries and directly connect our brains to the computer? Wouldn't it be easier and faster? That's the idea behind the brain–computer interface, the concept that lays the foundation for the technological telepathic superpowers.

"A brain-computer interface (BCI) is a computer-based system that acquires brain signals, analyzes them, and translates them into commands that are relayed to an output device to carry out a desired action" (Shih, Krusienski, and Wolpaw 2012). For example, a BCI detects the signals of a driver falling asleep behind the wheel, analyzes them to detect such drivers, and converts them into a meaningful output such as activating a vibrator in the seat to wake the driver up.

BCI is not a new phenomenon. Also referred to as brain–machine interface (BMI) or mind–machine interface (MMI), BCI has been around since the 1940s, even before the discovery of a computer, although coined only in the 1970s. The origins of BCI are deeply rooted in the medical field, with most of its uses still in the field to this date. BCI is being considered for uses outside the medical field only in the recent past.

The *Sunday Post* in April 2018 titled "Mind-Reading Headset Can Understand the Voice in Your Head" writes:

A team of researchers from MIT in the U.S. have created the AlterEgo, wearable tech which uses built-in electrodes to pick up neuromuscular signals in the user's jaw and face that are prompted by internal verbalization—or speaking "in your head." (Furmage 2018)

It is then able to translate these signals into words using AI and respond to commands in the same way as current virtual assistants. Although certain functions may require implanted devices, there has been tremendous investment in this field to eventually control machines through your thoughts. Watch this space.

Telepathy

"Two rats, about 3900 miles apart, cooperated on a task telepathically using their brain implants"—NBC News reported this development on February 28, 2013 (Subbaraman 2013). This experiment conducted by Duke University implanted brain chips in two rats, one located in North Carolina and the other in Brazil. The rats were trained to press a lever when a light went on above it. When they performed the task correctly, they got a drink of water.

The scientists conducting this experiment had the light only in one location, in this case, in the United States. When the light came on above the rat in the United States, the brain signal from this rat got transferred to the one in Brazil, and the rat in Brazil pulled the lever. The experiment also proved communication from the rat in Brazil to the one in the United States. When the rat in Brazil failed to pull the lever, the team didn't reward the rat in the United States. They noticed that the rat in the United States adjusted its behavior to make it easier for its partner to pull the lever this time.

The key takeaway from this experiment is that telepathy is not science fiction any longer. This technology has improved tremendously since this 2013 story. For example, Neuralink, Elon Musk's neurotechnology company, has been doing wonders, not only proving this technology is effective, but also safe. As of late 2022, they are in the process of getting ready to test these out on humans. If successful, the company claims that this technology can help people with paralysis, spinal injuries, Alzheimer's, and other yet-incurable diseases (Neate 2022).

The most important thing is this "brain chip" technology is bidirectional, meaning it helps output brain signals and inputs them, as seen with rats communicating across two different continents. Telepathic communication is a many-fold faster mode than conventional texting or touching and can soon become an everyday reality. If rats can do this today, humans can do this tomorrow.

Imagine a world where you think about someone, and she gets a ring tone inside her head. If the recipient accepts your call, both of you simply think of what to communicate. No more speaking on the phone. No more typing your messages. Dial someone inside your head and transfer your thoughts. Speaking to someone through that invisible Bluetooth headset in a crowded environment today confuses people around you so much. You can imagine how people around you would react when you think on those telepathic calls. This is how Falcon communicated with his brother Dragon on his way back from the doctor's office. The technology is in the beginning stages and it may be a while before such telepathy is enabled, but it is shaping up nicely. Although today's "brain chip" technology needs a brain implant, research is underway to make it less intrusive in the future.

You Become the Internet

A brain chip is a computer inside the head, similar to any other computer, just miniscule. We can call this a silicon-computer attached to our bio-computer, the brain. And this computer is connected to the outside world wirelessly. Until now, we have only discussed connecting the chip to other brains. What stops us from connecting this mini-computer inside our head to the vast Internet? Nothing. In fact, that would be an easier thing to do.

With access to the Internet, there will be endless opportunities. We would not need an Alexa or Siri any longer. We would have them inside our heads. We won't need our smartphone apps anymore. They'd be installed in our heads. Need to solve that complex math problem? The brain chip would compute it using Internet resources. Need to find the closest pizza place open in the middle of the night? Just ask the computer in your head. It will give you the results with a simple Internet search and take you there if you want. Your extended brain opens up a whole new world in the area of education and learning. Facts would be worthless to learn, worst to rote-learn. Knowledge will be so accessible that teachers *will* have to find analytical and creative ways to teach. If the Internet knows the answer, you know it. Conducting exams would have to turn those devices off mandatorily or at least restrict access to the Internet until then.

Essentially, you become the Internet; the Internet becomes you. This will enable the true merger of humans and machines. Some call this the further evolution of humans. They also depict this (not scientifically accurately though) in the form of monkeys evolving into apes, apes into humans, and humans into "humachines," also referred to as cyborgs. This will take some time, no doubt, especially for widespread adoption. But the technology is certainly evolving.

That's not the end, however. A brain will not only connect to the Internet, but multiple brains connect together to form a brain-net. What can all these connected brains do together? A lot. Take the example of the two rats again. Those rats were able to effectively communicate near-real-time and pass on crucial skills as well. What if a neuroscientist makes her brain entirely or partially open-source? You suddenly become a neuroscientist as well. If one swimmer in the world makes his swimming skill an open-source, you suddenly know how to swim as well. You can write computer programs if some computer programmer keeps her skill on this brain-cloud. You can fly an airplane if a pilot puts his brain on the brain-cloud. Suddenly you have access to skills you wouldn't have been able to gain in your lifetime.

Brain-net can be used not just to learn new skills, but for various other purposes. Teamwork and collaboration become more effective, as seen in the case of rats. Collective brainpower can be used to solve complex world problems. Important thoughts can be broadcasted to the masses. A reliable source can influence the public on important public measures, such as public health.

However, there are many shady sides to it, too. The government, for example, can get into people's heads to align or influence them to a desired task. This also comes with security risks. While the technology may be ready soon, it depends on how quickly we can make it safe for general consumption, whether the governments will allow it for general use, and how quickly people adopt it, among other factors.

We Will Continue to Play God

Thanks to genetic engineering, in human's pursuit to be on par with nature, we have created cats that glow in the dark, red strawberries with fish genes making them frost resistant, glow-in-the-dark rabbits, vitamin-A-rich golden rice, nutrient-rich veggies, bug-killing corn, non-browning apples, vitamin-rich super bananas, antioxidant-rich purple tomatoes, pollution-fighting plants, virus-resistant rainbow papaya, caterpillar-killing venomous cabbage, fast-growing Salmon, glittering-gold sea horses, singing mouse with bird genes, glowing fish, and many more. These are just a few examples of the products of genetic engineering.

November 29, 2018. James Gallagher writes in an article for the BBC: "He Jiankui shocked the world by claiming he altered the genes of twin baby girls so they could not contract HIV" (2019). Another news by the same source says: "Speaking to the Human Genome Editing Summit at the University of Hong Kong, [He Jiankui] said…[Lulu and Nana] were born normal and healthy, … there [are] plans to monitor the twins over the next 18 years." Lulu and Nana are the genetically modified twins.

Another news article on BBC News published in August 2020 reads:

> Florida mosquitoes: 750 million genetically modified insects to be released. The aim is to reduce the number of mosquitoes that carry diseases like dengue or the Zika virus. …the plan is to release the male, modified mosquitoes who will then hopefully breed with wild female mosquitoes. However, the males carry a protein that will kill off any female offspring before they reach mature biting age. Males, which only feed on nectar, will survive and pass on the genes. Over time, the aim is to reduce the population of *Aedes aegypti* mosquitoes in the area and thereby reduce the spread of disease to humans. (2020)

December 5, 2020. NBC News reported, "National Security Correspondent reports that China is conducting human tests to create biologically enhanced super soldiers" (Dilanian 2020). The details read: A top U.S. intelligence official says China has conducted human testing with hopes of developing soldiers with biologically enhanced capabilities. NBC's National Security Correspondent Ken Dilanian says, "Imagine a sniper who can see twice as far as a human being. Just the idea that China is studying these things is pretty troubling."

Let's have a look at one more example. Scientists at the University of Vermont have taken the cells from the embryos of a frog species and created new organisms through stem cell technology: "living robots" (Brown n.d.). They used a cluster of two types of cells: one type of cell that moves, that is, the heart cell, and the other, that doesn't. The contracting and expanding mechanism were exploited through their cell DNA and were used to create motion, similar to what a motor would create, but obviously a slow one. A bunch of these heart cells and skin cells were arranged in an optimal fashion to form a new living organism that can swim with these heart muscle cells and carry small loads such as medicine through a hole in their structure. This is not reprogramming the DNA of any existing species. This is not the creation of a mechanical robot. This is not even the regeneration of cells in our body. This is the creation of a new species altogether, a living organism. Isn't that amazing? This organism is said to have enough protein inside of it to survive for a week. Moreover, in a protein-rich environment, it's said to last longer, similar to any other living being. This organic bot can heal itself if damaged. And once dead, this organic bot turns into dead cells.

We are only beginning to scratch the surface of what biotechnology and genetic engineering has to offer. We will beat several genetic diseases, such as retinitis pigmentosa, sickle cell disease, and Down syndrome. We will truly be able to "play God" to adjust our genetic code. This technology can also be used to enhance your abilities and turn you into a superhuman, as it was allegedly done in the case of Chinese soldiers.

Our first few ancestors walked on all four. The quadruped humans became bipedal through millions of years of evolution. Evolution simply means rewriting the source code—the genome sequence—that produces all of us. The source code is adjusted to adapt to the natural conditions and passed on to the next generation. However, this process is so slow, no living being lives to see it.

But when science has given us the ability to tweak into the biological source code, should we accelerate or slow the evolution altogether? Instead of waiting another million years through the natural evolution to grow that third eye at the back of our head, what if we are able to figure out a way to modify our DNA to do that instantly? Will we produce designer babies?

The question is not whether it is possible, but whether it is ethical and, most importantly, safe. As much hope genetic engineering offers in solving some of our most critical problems, it also has some dangerous possibilities. There are indeed several social and ethical questions associated with it; the risks this technology poses are far more dangerous, ranging from designer babies experiments going wrong all the way to purposefully creating bioweapons that can erase a portion of humankind or rogue leaders forcing the formation of a certain race to exhibit race superiority. The ethicality of this pursuit is certainly debatable. But at the same time, it is also true that what is seemingly possible *will* be made possible, if not by one, then the other.

To summarize, I see us continue to play God, but at a slow, but steady pace. This area is strictly regulated by several governments around the world and also by international agreements. However, if we use our modified version of Murphy's law, "If something is possible, it will eventually happen," someone somewhere will use genetic engineering in their self-interest. We should all be prepared for it.

You Can Live Forever If You Choose

Let's say you hire someone to make your robotic look-alike—call it Canopus—a humanoid with almost identical somatic features as yours, though not a clone.

Now, using the brain-chip technology, what if we map your brain's computational network and memories, upload it on a drive, and download them onto your robotic look-alike to engineer a robotic twin? Canopus could have your voice as well. We have your twin ready that looks like you, talks like you, and acts like you, only immortal. Your robotic twin could live forever, provided it is regularly serviced. Pixel, Falcon's mom in our tale, is one such mind-upload.

This certainly brings several questions to the table, as any new technology does. If the mind-upload onto another robot or even human is possible, who and what else can we upload our minds onto? Onto an animal? Granted, the "hardware" or the animal brain circuitry may not be compatible with the software, that is, your brain map. But if we develop a compatibility-enabling software, those sci-fi feats they show in movies will come true: we might actually have a cross-conscious species, an animal-human. Possibilities are as many as your imagination: What if we upload our minds into some weird-looking machines? What about a car with a human mind? What about an unnerving, giant, sturdy metallic robot with *your* mind?

However, are we counting too much on the brain-chip technology? What if the brain-chip technology fails to deliver this mind content extraction? Will that be the end of this dream of technological immortality? Can we employ the currently available technology instead of relying on something that is under development? There's a way out; though it is not a full-proof solution, there is a way to create our replicas.

Let me ask you a question. "Who knows you the most?" Your mom? Your dad? Your spouse? Your sibling? Your best friend? Or yourself? Nobody knows me better than myself. All of that may be true, but in the past. Someone—or rather something—spying on you all day and night probably knows the most about you, even better than yourself? It's the Internet. Let's call him Mr. I.

Mr. I knows how you look because it has your pictures you uploaded on social media, shared through those chat applications, or even through e-mails. He knows where you live, which school you went to, whether you're married, what you do, if you have kids, which school your kids go to, who your friends are, who your spouse's friends are, who your best friends are, who your neighbors are, your direct family details, your extended family details, your daily activities, including their locations, and hundreds of other answers. But this is nothing compared to who you stalk, who stalks on you, what are your fantasies, what your pass time is, what medicine you're taking, what's your mood, which political party you belong to, whether you're angry today, among others. You are in Mr. I's fingertips.

You liked and disliked some posts on social media or commented on them. You followed people, joined groups, and watched videos based on your interests. You shopped several products on the Internet. Mr. I has your entire online shopping history. Even if you use your credit card for purchases in stores and not online, you left a trail for Mr. I to follow. Mr. I will track your expenses.

If you are one of the very few who uses cash, you make it harder for Mr. I to paw you, but he can still figure it out. For example, most of us research on the things we want to buy online before heading over to a store, unless they are smaller day-to-day items. You already told Mr. I what you like. If you extensively researched on a washing machine of brand "A" for a few weeks, read its online reviews, spent more time on clicking on links related to its particular model, and, all of a sudden, stopped doing any research on washing machines, Mr. I can assume with some level of certainty that you bought that particular model of washing machine, even if you paid cash. You make it easier for Mr. I if immediately after stopping to search for "which brand is the best," you instead search "why does my washing machine smell." Another way Mr. I knows you bought that washing machine is by tracking your cash withdrawal pattern to match with the cost of the washing machine to confirm its assumption. Mr. I will be fully laid back to enjoy your purchase confirmation if you post about your new washing helper on the social media.

Using all these data, Mr. I can easily formulate your profile drawing from the information you gave: your likes, dislikes, and interests. Mr. I, through his advanced AI algorithms, can predict how you respond to various situations. For example, if you consistently commented positively (with positive word connotations) on pro-choice-related posts, it's clear you are "pro-choice." Even if you don't comment and just read them, your level of engagement with the content tells Mr. I how interested you are in the topic. Add your video-watching habits to it. If you are "pro-choice," it is likely you'll watch pro-liberal videos. Depending on the amount of time you spend on pro-choice versus pro-life posts and their comments, Mr. I can come to a reasonable conclusion on your viewpoint, if not the first time, but upon reading patterns of your behavior. All of this is possible, only if you allow Mr. I to track you, although most of us enable these features knowingly or unknowingly.

These are only meant to be examples of how every move you make on the Internet leaves digital bread crumbs for Mr. I to pick up, put pieces together, form the whole, and read your mind. Let's take a few more examples. You checked in and out of various places you visit on social media. You created posts from those places. You used maps to get to your destinations. You drove your car that knows where you go and at what time. This became easier with smart cars. You used telepay applications in various places. You did some research on Google to find places you wanted to visit at various times of the day or the week. You checked for weather before you wanted to go out. Using an AI algorithm, Mr. I will be able to put together your entire daily, weekly, monthly, and even yearly schedule, even better than you can do it.

You share your emotions on the Internet. You tell random people when you are happy, sad, angry, or feel low. Even if you don't explicitly express your feelings, your video-watching patterns, search patterns, and shopping patterns can tell your mood. What made it even easier? Personal assistants such as Alexa. You ask Alexa to play relaxation music when you are stressed. Songs with dance beat when you are happy. That mood can easily be mapped to the other activity, snippets of which you leave on the Internet. For example, when you are stressed, you may end up taking a nap or you may go to the gym. You may eat out or go small-shopping when you are happy. You may go big-shopping if you are super happy. There is mapping of mood to weather patterns, geopolitical events, economy, and so on, over patterns of our behaviors. The point is: each one of us is so predictable even though we consider ourselves as the most unpredictable.

Putting all these together, Mr. I can easily map your brain and create your digital twin. The interesting thing is: it will create your persona better than you can because you do a lot of these activities through your subconscious mind. Your mind profile, as collected by Mr. I, can be uploaded onto your robotic look-alike to create your robotic twin that will share your interests, the one that will think and behave like you.

Your twin will not get everything right. However, the AI algorithm Mr. I added to your twin's brain will learn as it goes, to fill any gaps. A good example of this was how Pixel learned what happened when her memory was erased in Falcon's tale. The AI can persuade others to provide that missing information and learn from it. If our mind is what defines us, did we just recreate ourselves into an immortal version? However, there is one major missing piece here, that is, consciousness. The problem with consciousness is that it is as difficult to define as to achieve. Lately, there have been multiple philosophers and scientists writing books, one after the other, in consciousness raising further questions than answering the existing. After all, the axiom seems to be true—the more books are published on a topic, the less people understand what it is. Other than that, today's Mr. I can recreate you and give you a technological immortality. And who knows where the field of artificial consciousness is headed in the coming years.

Internet Connectivity Through Space

I went to a boarding school around 800 km away from home in a small town called Nagarjunasagar, India, to complete my high school in the 1990s. I still remember how we gathered and waited for the postman every afternoon, hoping we would get a letter from home, which my parents wrote and posted. These letters took days to arrive. By the time I would have responded, the letter would have taken almost 10 days to do a round trip. Urgent messages were sent using telegram. It took hours to reach, instead of days, but that used to be expensive and limited to serious, emergency messages. Telephone was a remote idea to us.

Fast forward a few years. I went to another boarding school in the northern part of India in a town called Pilani for my undergraduate studies. While connectivity was still not widespread, we had access to telephones. My parents would call on a public phone once in a while and we would chat for a few minutes. That was a major upgrade from the previous modes of communication.

Slowly, Internet became available in the early 21st century, but its availability was extremely limited. This was back in India and I know

Internet was available in the United States during the last quarter of the 20th century. However, we had to make a trip to an Internet cafe and pay per minute to use it, which ran, as we all know, at snail's pace. It was predominantly dial-up based and in-home Internet was limited to a few major cities at a premium price.

Today, broadband Internet is widely available in many parts of the world. We rely less on cable TV, depend more on video streaming for entertainment. Compare today's Internet speeds of few to thousands of mbps to back in the day. We made a significant stride, all thanks to fiber optic-enabled broadband Internet cable installed in several parts of the globe.

However, this story only applies to well-developed areas of the world. The speeds are much lower in a large chunk of population with an estimated 37 percent of the world—2.9 billion people—still without Internet connectivity, an international telecommunication report says (2021). We don't have to go far to understand this. The evidences may be intertwined within our experiences. My wife and I own a vacation rental space in the Lake Tahoe area, not underdeveloped by any means, but there is no broadband connectivity. Our guests constantly complain about the lack of Internet access.

However, the good news is: this is all about to change. The world will likely and soon get consistent Internet access in its every corner.

SpaceX is planning to send 42,000 satellites as a part of its Starlink initiative to provide high-speed Internet to every corner of the world, from forests to poles (Mann, Pultarova, and Howell 2022). Kuiper Systems LLC, a subsidiary of Amazon (sister company of Blue Origin), has received approval to launch more than 3,000 satellites with the same goal (Smith 2022). The advanced space technology made satellite launching much easier as compared to even a few years ago; we will see exponential growth in the number of satellites orbiting us, providing global connectivity like never before. Starlink Beta has already been launched and has been taking reservations for satellite-based high-speed Internet. Our world will soon become truly connected from North Pole to South Pole and all around, meeting the heightened connectivity needs of future "things" alongside humans.

Smart Tablets Are the Future

Your reaction would probably be: tablets are already smart. I have a smart iPad and my friend has a Samsung Galaxy Tab. They are just bigger smartphones.

I am not referring to those tablets. I am talking about pills. Yes, the pills we swallow. What if those pills become smart? These smart pills are the future of medicine. In the story you read, Falcon took a pill that diagnosed the issue that allowed Pixel to 3D-print the medicine for him. That is a smart pill.

Smart pills do exist today and we're not in a movie script.

No, not on the dark market.

Not in any country with an authoritarian rule where it's easy to impose such things on people.

What if doctors in the United States can prescribe a smart pill for patients, fully approved by the U.S. Food and Drug Administration (FDA)? This is already happening. Susan Scutti writes for the CNN:

> FDA approves pill with digital tracking device you swallow: A psychiatric medication system in the form of a pill with a built-in digital tracking device gained approval from the U.S. Food and Drug Administration on Monday. Abilify MyCite, a form of arip-iprazole and a first-of-its-kind product, has an embedded ingest-ible sensor that records when the medication is taken. Made by Japan-based Otsuka Pharmaceutical Co., the medication system is intended to treat schizophrenia, bipolar 1 disorder, and depression in adults. (Scutti 2017)

This is where I believe the future of medicine is headed. Let's say you have flu-like symptoms. You take a "smart" pill connected to your smart-phone. It may contain nanobots made of, say, metals, nonmetals, or pro-teins that do their job and come out the next morning when you use the restroom or, even better, dissolve inside your body—biodegradable xenobots. Their job is to analyze the problem and make a diagnosis. They will be able to check your blood sugar levels, detect bacteria, search for viral DNA, and even do a biopsy. They transmit their findings to the smartphone that triggers the 3D printer that can print the actual pill based on the diagnosis. Your doctor's office will be notified on all this, provided you authorize it. How does this future of curative medicine sound?

Now, let's extend these smart pills to preventive care. What if you periodically take a smart pill that does an end-to-end body checkup and sends the results back to your smartphone as well as the doctor's office? The idea is very similar to annual checkups but without blood work, urine tests, and long anxious anticipation times—the annual checkup in a pill, essentially. All good, if there is nothing wrong. If the issues are minor, your smartphone can give you a treatment plan using an advanced FDA-approved AI algorithm, and an FDA-approved 3D printer will print the designated medicine for you. If the issue is serious, you go to see a doctor. Sounds good?

Back to the pills: what if these smart pills or intravenous fluids enter our body, identify cell damages proactively through advanced AI algorithms, and repair them or assess for a treatment plan such as proactive stem cell therapy? Your heart cells are wearing out. The bots can detect them early. All you need to do is grow their clone in the lab to produce new ones. The same will be true for other organs. Wouldn't that improve the quality of our life or even reverse aging? We may or may not be able to live for 500 years like those sharks, but wouldn't it be a huge win if we can expand our life span?

In extension, these smart pills or injections filled with nanobots can go and repair all kinds of bodily damages. For instance, they can clear plaque on the walls of our arteries or tear up a clot. This is the future of medicine and all the excitement lies right at the intersection of biotechnology and high technology.

Magic Cell, Not Magic Pill

Diseases such as cancer, diabetes, heart disorders, and Alzheimer's have been tied to aging and premature death for a long time. These diseases take millions of lives each year. According to WHO, ischemic heart disease, stroke, and chronic obstructive pulmonary disease (COPD) were the top three causes of death in 2019 (2020). For years, we've tried to control them but couldn't eliminate their risks altogether. What does the future hold? Can we eradicate these diseases like we eradicated smallpox? You probably are aware of someone who would have been alive today had we figured out a way to cure their diseases.

Can a diabetic patient eat what she likes without having to worry about shooting up her blood sugar levels? Would a heart patient be able to live peacefully without having to worry every day? Can cancer patients live a normal life without having to go through those painful chemotherapies? Can improved cognition capabilities help do things without assistance? The point is: the quality of life would drastically improve.

How about developing a magic pill that cures these ailments? Here you have to present your idea of why magic pill won't work.

Let's get to the point. I believe the future lies not in magic pills, but magic cells. These cells are named stem cells. Part of what is called regenerative medicine—a medical field that uses our body's own healing process to cure diseases—the stem cell therapy holds significant promises to curing diseased organs without extreme intervention.

Have you ever gotten injured? I am sure you had at least one instance of a paper cut or some other injury to your skin. Did it heal? How long did it take? Your skin healed because the cells regenerated, thanks to your stem cells. If we break our bones, they will rejoin. Our body constantly produces new blood. Your body contains enormous healing power. Stem cell therapy uses this power to treat serious diseases.

The Promise of mRNA Vaccines

The history of human civilization is riddled with pandemics, each one leaving a trail of death and destruction in its wake. From the 1918 Spanish Flu to the 2020 COVID-19 pandemic, the threat of infectious diseases has been a constant companion to humanity.

One of the most devastating of these was the 1918 Spanish Flu, which claimed an estimated 50 million lives worldwide and a quarter of the world's population. Even more recent outbreaks, such as the 1968 Hong Kong flu pandemic and the 1967 influenza A (H2N2) virus, claimed millions of lives. And let's not forget the devastating impact of pandemics such as AIDS, cholera, bubonic plague, and the ongoing cancer epidemic. These outbreaks have not only claimed countless lives, but also left distressing trails of warnings for humanity. The 2005 bird flu caused by

H5N1, once estimated to kill up to 150 million people if not contained, is a chilling reminder of the constant threat of pandemics.

In the face of these deadly outbreaks, one of the most promising new technologies in this field is mRNA technology. Unlike traditional vaccines, which use the pathogen itself to generate an immune response, mRNA vaccines work by instructing the body to create the spike protein of the virus, which is then recognized by the immune system as foreign. This approach has been proven to be both effective and adaptable, as creating a booster for various COVID variants has been proven much simpler than conventional methods. The use of bioinformatics and AI has further streamlined the process and increased its effectiveness.

However, this technology is not limited to COVID-19. Research is currently underway to develop mRNA vaccines for a wide range of viruses and bacteria, including other coronaviruses, influenza, HIV, herpes, and malaria. Additionally, mRNA technology is being explored as a treatment for diseases such as cancer and cystic fibrosis, as well as for gene therapy to repair defective genes.

Furthermore, mRNA technology will also be used to treat existing diseases like cancer that will teach the immune system to attack malignant cells. This technology could also be used to repair defective genes to treat diseases such as cystic fibrosis. For instance, Penn Medicine researchers are using mRNA technology to modify liver genes, thereby permanently reducing cholesterol levels and protecting against heart attack and stroke (*Source*: Pennmedicine.org. 2021. "World-Changing mRNA Vaccines From Penn Medicine." www.pennmedicine.org/mrna (accessed January 14, 2023).

In short, the future of vaccinology is looking bright. mRNA technology has proven to be a powerful and adaptable tool in the fight against infectious diseases, and its potential applications are far-reaching. With ongoing research and development, we may be able to create a world where pandemics are a thing of the past.

Inorganic Workers

We've seen how AI has been advancing and will continue to advance, along IoT. There is a parallel field witnessing an equal growth—the world of robotics. Robots are extensively used in factories to perform various manufacturing and assembly tasks. Those inorganic factory workers will only multiply and become smarter.

The domestic and institutional use of robots is a growing trend. We can expect these inorganic workers to rapidly replace humans everywhere. From self-checkout store counters to humanless parking systems, this is already happening. Let's take a few more examples.

Amazon Go is a completely human-free retail grocery store. You can walk into it, pick things up, and walk out. Your activity is tracked through advanced facial recognition and IoT sensors. You will be charged automatically, and the bill will be sent to you after your visit. This is seen as a model for future retail stores. According to Scrapehero.com, there are 27 of them active as of July 15, 2022 (2022).

There is a completely human-free coffee shop in San Francisco where robots prepare coffee. The international airport in Seoul, South Korea, is full of guide robots roaming around. They inform and escort you to different places within the airport, such as bathrooms, shops, and other areas. When they walk ahead, remember to follow them.

There are fully automatic hotels in China operated by bots. Several modern restaurants in Beijing use robots to bring food to the table. There is at least one fully automated restaurant where robots take order, prepare food, and even deliver them. Humans are present, but their job is to provide a personal touch for the customer experience.

Our roads will soon fill with robots in the form of autonomous vehicles. Stores will be full of robots working the shelves, taking payments, and providing guidance inside. Airways will witness more flying robots, in the form of drones and air taxis. We already have arguably the biggest robots in our airways—airplanes. When in autopilot mode, an airplane is nothing but a colossal, flying robot capable of carrying people. These carrying robots will transport people and things to space in the form of spacecraft and ferry them underground through underground technologies, for instance, the Hyperloop and other technologies. Our waterways will carry autonomous yachts or water robots as well. A baby version is the Tesla Model Y Super Yacht. And finally at home, we already have digital assistant robots like Alexa and vacuum cleaner robots like Roomba. Not very distant in time, Tesla's bot might also join with promises of its own. Our lives will be filled with more of these robots, as they did in Falcon's life.

You Will Soon Become a Cyborg

I am a cyborg. I love technology so much that I turned myself into a cyborg. And be prepared to hear when and why I turned into a cyborg. No, it was not when Elon Musk started Neuralink which you might already suspect because of my repeated mentions of his companies. But that's just a reportage of the ones in the forefront.

I have been a cyborg since my childhood, and I can say it is not a dream by any means.

Perhaps, we should define the term cyborg first. I became a cyborg the day I received a calculator.

My point is we are all already cyborgs, as long as we use some sort of technology to improve our natural abilities. Yes, you are a cyborg, as long as you use a phone, computer, or any other technology. The calculator enhanced my math skills tremendously. My smartphone not only gives me information the most powerful person on the earth could only imagine getting a few decades ago, but it also lets me control my home and the world on my palm.

We are all convertible cyborgs, meaning when we use our smartphones, we become one. Yes, we're detachable. We are cyborgs when we wear our glasses or contact lens and convert back to our normal state when we stop using them. What if we start becoming permanent cyborgs of some sort? What does that even mean? That simply means we implant technology in our bodies to enhance our abilities.

But these technologies only turn us into a one-major-step-away cyborgs. And that major step is the biomechatronics—the marriage of biology with mechanical science. True cyborgs are biomechatronic organisms with deep levels of human–machine interaction.

The brain-chip we discussed earlier makes us a "true" cyborg. But we don't have to go that far. Humans have been medically turned into cyborgs as early as 1960s when the first pacemaker was invented. If you've met someone who has a pacemaker, you've met a cyborg. Anyone with an artificial body part is a permanent cyborg. The interesting aspect of this topic is how this field is progressing.

Let's review this 2016 NBC story:

"Brain Chip Helps Paralyzed Man Feel His Fingers" (Fox 2016). "Nathan Copeland, paralyzed from the chest down for 12 years, can feel his fingers again. And he fist-bumped President Obama with a robotic hand."

Copeland had been paralyzed from the waist down. The University of Pittsburg implanted a brain-chip to read his thoughts through brain signals, interpreted them through AI, transferred them over to a robotic arm, and put his thoughts to action through it. Brain implants are beyond animal-based experiments and are being used on humans already.

The brain-chip technology has promising benefits. Artificial hands and eyes connected to the brain through interfaces are just examples. The prospects this area offers are fascinating. For example, humans are in a dire need of eyes with an ability to detect wavelengths normal eyes cannot. Do you feel like flying in the air like a bird? No problem. Brain-chip technology through gaining control of our brain offers hope that you can attach synthetic wings that can be connected to your brain one day. Do you want to become invisible? That's possible, too, except that we don't need to wait long for this fiction to become a reality. "Harry Potter"-style invisible blankets are available today, although they have some Is to dot and Ts to cross. While they are being developed for use by the soldiers at the moment, it doesn't look like it will be long before I can order my magic blanket you can hide in from Amazon. Not sure what I would do with it, but I guess it will be a cool thing to at least play around with.

The Future Is All About Space

You probably might have heard of the space race of the 20th century, especially the Sputnik Moment of 1957, the first one ever, named after the satellite Sputnik 1, Earth's first artificial satellite launched into orbit by the Soviet Union. Sputnik 1 marked the beginning of the space era. The space race became so historical that the term Sputnik Moment is now commonly used for the need to catch up with major breakthroughs, especially brought about by other countries or societies. The United States decided to catch up to this space race and landed a man on

Moon in 1969. Twentieth century was an era of space race between the political powers.

Space exploration was fully owned and executed by governments or its bodies, for instance, NASA in the United States, which started back in the 20th century. The nature of space exploration has completely changed in the 21st century, with private companies actively participating or even leading in the process. Some media outlets characterize the current space exploration initiatives as the "space race of the billionaires," although I do not agree with that characterization. Multibillionaire entrepreneurs are investing their fortunes in space exploration, and that's a very good thing.

Steve Gorman reported for the Reuters on July 12, 2021: "Billionaire Branson Soars to Space Aboard Virgin Galactic Flight" (2021). Another such news by Reuters reports Jeff Bezos' success in flying 66.5 miles (107 km) above the Texas desert in his company Blue Origin's Shepard launch vehicle (Johnson 2021). The vehicle returned back to earth safely after taking "a historic suborbital flight." The key here is the safe return back to earth, which was not possible before. Although these missions barely touched the space, they mark a new era in the world of space race.

According to Boeing, "Space industry is expected to be a total $2.6 trillion market this decade. The United States represents nearly 60 percent of the total market, with the rest coming from allied nations around the world." We are undoubtedly entering the never-seen-before space era. The investments pouring into space missions seem to substantiate this story. Billionaires around the world are literalizing the catchphrase: follow the money and so should the common man, as far as possible and ethical.

NASA's next lunar mission aims to launch the first woman and the first person of color to the moon (Gohd 2021). Artemis missions, as it's called, plans to "establish the first long-term presence on the moon," learn from these endeavors, and finally use that knowledge to send the first astronauts to Mars (2022). Watch this "SPACE."

Your Car Is the Next Cash Cow

The east valley of Phoenix, Arizona, United States.

You open your smartphone app and request a taxi. It comes to you in within minutes. You get in and settle down. The driver greets you. You greet him back. You get busy with your phone, watching your favorite

Netflix show. The car starts moving toward your destination. The driver drives you to the destination very carefully, following all the traffic laws and lights. He maintains all the speed limits, evades the traffic around him, slows down at speed bumps, stops for any pedestrians crossing the road, and safely takes you to your destination.

You had one of the best driving experiences and are impressed. You thank the driver for such a wonderful ride and wrongfully extend your hand for a handshake. But you realize there's no one in the driving seat. The 1s and 0s are the driver: say hello to Google Waymo, the smart, electric, autonomous "ghost" driver in town.

Another artificially intelligent "ghost" already dominating the domestic market is Tesla with many more existing and upcoming players.

We already had a lot of car talk thus far in this chapter. Let's do some more, especially summarizing the future of cars. Three letters S-E-A describe the future of cars: smart, electric, and autonomous.

Smart

With minor connectivity options as of 2022, in the years to come, your car will be able to connect to other machines, talk to other cars and traffic lights on the road, shop for you, and make all the payments autonomously (with your permission) to provide a coordinated experience. This includes paying your bills, reminding you of upcoming appointments, and even making appointments for you, like a personal assistant. You can talk and argue with your car. If it wins, it will play your favorite music to calm you down. Most new features will come to you through updates. Your car will have a digital twin and she will be smart enough to ensure you reach your destination effectively and safely.

Electric

As a part of the green revolution, there is a constant push to reduce our dependency on fossil fuels and thus promote renewable sources of energy. Electric-powered cars are already the future and there's no stopping their sales. In August 2021, American President Biden signed an order "aiming for half of all new vehicles sold by 2030 to be electric powered"

(Ewing 2021). It said, "Automakers' expected quick transition from gas-burning cars and trucks to electric is a key part of the White House strategy to fight global warming"—NBC News reported (Lederman 2021). Almost 95.4 percent cars on the streets of the United States are gas-run and only 4.6 percent are plug-in electric vehicles (Blanco 2022). The dream of replacing fossil fuel with electric cars and lessening the carbon burden in the atmosphere needs to invert the 95.4 percent to 4.6 percent statistics of their respective distribution. You will have time to transition, although gas-based cars are not entirely going away. The current clean energy push is for new cars and by the way it's progressing, one can safely predict that the transition will happen over decades, not merely in few years.

Autonomous

My Tesla—we named it "The Autonomous Vanka"—drives herself in most circumstances and is a great relief for people like me who don't enjoy driving, especially long distances. I just sit behind the wheel, punch in the destination, and she does most of the work. But today's Tesla still requires the driver to be behind the wheel, just like how airplanes still require the pilot to be there, although airplanes are autonomous for the most part. The future cars will be completely self-driving. The technology in the car is ready for the most part, although it will continue to improve. The part that needs revamping, and is the longest pole in the tent, is the infrastructure to support autonomous cars such as smart signaling lights and smart roads compatible for autonomous cars. There is already a huge push for that and the growing number of patents indicates things are promising.

Think about what an autonomous car can do. It will take the "Uber revolution" to an entirely new level, transporting people and cargo autonomously everywhere. Your car will drop you off at your workplace or the shopping mall and immediately can go work as a taxi when you don't need her, making you some extra cash. In the long run, your car will not be a depreciating liability but a growing asset. Future cars will travel on the road by detecting other cars and things through a direct connectivity through IoT as compared to today's computer vision and other sensors. For example, your car will slow down because she knows that Deaver's car is right in front of her and is about to slow down through direct communication between the two. She will stop at the traffic light not because she read the light through computer vision, but she has been notified of the red light directly by the traffic light IoT sensor, again through direct communication. That's the future of transportation connectivity.

Travel to an Alternate World in a Split Second

Getting bored of our day-to-day life happens occasionally for all of us and that's entirely normal. Back in the day, our ancestors talked to each other to kill their boredom, meaning, they used to immerse themselves into a different world through communication. Then came the time when people read books in addition to simply talking to other people, followed by pictures and videos, from black and white to "kind of" color to full color. The quality of this colored motion picture significantly evolved over time, taking forms such as high definition and blue ray. We have 3D motion pictures that take us a bit closer to reality, creating an "immersive" experience. In addition, some theaters add dimensions of seat movements and climactic controls and take it to a whole new level.

But these technologies struggle to bridge the gap between the physical and virtual worlds completely. The 21st-century technology that gives us a closer, native feeling of reality is called virtual reality (VR). If it's developed right, you won't be able to tell the difference between the real world and the VR world. That's why it's called virtual "reality." Although the definition is evolving, this merger of the physical and virtual worlds is also known as the metaverse. The selfies you take on your cellphone morphing your face is a primitive example of the metaverse in action.

It's a given that the future of gaming and entertainment is in the hands of VR. However, there is much more to it. Imagine attending a school field trip from your home without moving an inch. When this world will look as real as the real world, why not just attend it from the comfort of your bed? Most of the future field training will be through VR, avoiding all the dangers of the real world. Beyond training, you could also operate heavy machinery belonging to the dangerous field from the comfort of your desk, without the physical dangers in its virtual digital twin. Future work-meetings could be remote, bringing all the participants into a virtual meeting room in the metaverse. Online shopping experience will significantly improve through at-home trial rooms. You can do several tasks at home, those you need to go out to do. The gap between the virtual and the real worlds will significantly reduce, allowing you to switch back and forth in no time.

Web 3.0 May Not Be What Everyone Imagines

Web 3.0 is a buzz word that is going viral lately. First, what is it? While this is just an idea at the moment and is evolving, the concept calls for democratization of the Internet. Web 1.0: Internet in its early days was mostly a one-way communication tool through publishing of information on websites that was consumed by users. Advances on the Internet gave rise to Web 2.0 where interactions with the Internet became common through the likes of social media. The idea is that the World Wide Web will evolve further into version 3.0 where the Internet will be democratized and everyone will profit from it. How?

First, the data will be decentralized through blockchain as compared to sitting in Big Tech's data center. You control your data and sell them if you want. Your every action on the Internet could make you money. The argument is that this will also be secure. Second, beyond selling your data, you also participate on the Internet to make money by doing what you like, such as playing video games or showing your other talents to your followers. It will all be controlled through blockchain technology and the financial medium through which you make the money: cryptocurrency.

The current definition of Web 3.0 was coined with cryptocurrency in mind and it has been embraced by crypto enthusiasts. I am not sure how successful that will be. More on crypto coming up under the future of money. Besides, I don't believe we are ready yet to move our Internet completely onto blockchain technology. Performance will be one of the roadblocks.

However, I absolutely see the fundamentals behind Web 3.0 materializing, that is, taking control of your data and profiting from the

Internet. While it may not happen through democratization of the maintenance of data through technologies such as blockchain, there will be more transparency in how our data are managed by organizations, driven by competition, public demand, and perhaps through regulations. Remember, sitting on a gold mine we discussed earlier? Profiting from our data is absolutely in the near future. Coming to profiting off our talents? Isn't that happening already? Content providers get paid off the views and likes on YouTube. Some influencers make millions. Some video gamers live off playing games. See these trends grow by not only getting paid for more activities on the Internet—post engagements and so on as examples, but also expect more transparency.

Bored of This World? Move to a Different One

Our world used to be small in the past, about 2.5 million years ago. People lived in small caves or basic huts and would only go out for primal needs. They hunted and gathered using sharpened stones and bones. They searched for food on land and in water and fed on what was already there in nature.

Slowly, they felt the need for more sophisticated tools and a need to leave home for survival. After millions of years, they were able to extend their march from their cave-home to across the oceans. And the rest is known.

Our presumptions have been repeatedly shattered. We thought the sun was the biggest. It rather turned out to be average in size. We thought the sun was alone until we found billions of other stars. We thought our galaxy was alone until billions of other galaxies shimmered in the eyes of the telescopes like sand particles. Now we're left with one "truth" and it is one of the most consistently held "truth" that hasn't been shattered yet: our position in the universe. What if we're wrong, again? What if we're not alone?

This exact feeling fuels our drive for surfing through the space in the early attempts of dominating it. Space travel, space economy, and Internet connectivity are just a few immediate benefits we will be experiencing here on the earth, directly resulting in this space race. But as clearly stated by a lot of these missions, the eventual goal is to make humans a multiplanetary species. It will be unwise on our part not to discuss this or act on it. The space is massive and there are lots of opportunities to make a place our home, just a little challenging.

Where will we eventually build our new home in space? Will we colonize the Moon? Will our children play on Mars? This question lingers in the minds of a lot of people.

Our ancestors thousands of years ago migrated from Africa to Asia, Europe (Gugliotta 2008), and eventually to the entire planet (well, pretty much). The question we are asking on space colonization here is similar to asking our ancestors where they were planning to settle when they first started off. They had no clue that thousands of years later their subsequent generations would colonize a place and make it today's America. While it's not entirely clear, scientists have the consensus that humans started out in Africa and the trigger for migration was a scarcity of resources such as food, amid a growing population. Sounds familiar?

The case is similar for space colonization. The current space colonization is in the exact same spot as the case for early human migration from Africa. We can only discuss our first destination, driven by the most pragmatic, immediate options. But there's a significant difference in motive for major changes between the ancient era and today. First, scientific innovations, today, are not just driven by genuine, collective human needs, but also a need to be superior in terms of resources. Second, more than the needs, they're driven by whether it's commercially feasible in short, fairly long, or long-term scenario. So, predicting the human space journey is not that difficult provided the options we have.

Despite all the energies, space settlements are not going to be a one-time event but a continuous process with ever-growing expansion. And it's not going to happen overnight. The first settlement, wherever it ends up happening, is important, and that immediate goal is what the key stakeholders involved in space exploration are referring to. The sky is the limit from there; well, perhaps I should say the space is the limit instead, as we continue to expand our footprint into the infinitely large void of the universe.

The Moon

Being the closest giant rocky structure, it's not a surprise that Moon has been human's spatial holy grail for a while now. As mentioned, NASA is planning the next mission to Moon with a goal to send humans by around 2024, this time to stay and explore.

The question is—what do we do when we land there? There will certainly be further exploration to determine what can and cannot be done because we know very little about Moon even though we've been there a couple of times.

But one thing we know for sure is that Moon doesn't have an atmosphere, unlike Earth, and with it arises two major risks: dangerous radiation exposure and lack of oxygen. The primary goal is not to die and definitely not by radiation because that's the most widely known risk. Also, on a lighter note, moving to the Moon will prove to be the best diet plan: it will be the fastest way to lose one-sixth of your weight because the gravity of the moon is approximately one-sixth of the Earth's.

But, in all seriousness, questions we do not have answers to include how abundant frozen water is there on (inside?) the Moon. There are signs that the water is more abundant than we originally thought. We have many signs of underground lava tunnels. Once we explore them further, they may be ideal options for our first lunar colonies. There is definitely a lot of work to be done such as figuring out a way to set up solar plants, but we are getting closer to making our way to the Moon, not just to plant a flag but to settle down this time.

The Mars

If you're someone who loves science and movies, chances are you know about Mars exploration missions, especially in the last few decades, led by NASA and other agencies.

Mars' atmosphere is thinner compared to Earth but thicker than that of the Moon, making it slightly a better option to colonize. Bad news for those with quick weight loss ambitions: you would only lose two-thirds of your weight on Mars, compared to five-sixths on Moon. But extreme care should be taken not to opt for the Mars mission just to see your weight reduced, by the way.

Scientists have already found signs of water, including large amounts of underground ice. Ancient Mars had the right chemistry to support living microbes, including the existence of sulfur, nitrogen, oxygen, phosphorus, and carbon—key ingredients necessary for life.

Futurists out there have created a blueprint to reach Mars, including a plan to run shuttles back and forth between Mars and Earth. We have identified an ideal location to start our Mars colony along with a blueprint to build dome-like structures, with detailed interior designs. We planned out the type of food to carry, plants to grow, and eventually atmosphere to nurture which doesn't require us to live inside dome-like structures at all times. *Welcome to Mars* by Buzz Aldrin has outlined these plans. Strap yourself for the journey Earthlings!

However, we still do not know a lot about Mars, more so than the Moon. The Martian lava tubes may be a better choice for human explorer colonies; we will only find out once we reach there. They essentially act as natural domes protecting from space radiation more than artificial structures. The longer-term solution is to build an Earth-like atmosphere on Mars that would naturally block the lethal radiation.

But how do we do it? Scientists are exploring several options. One option is to develop greenhouse gas factories. These are the same greenhouse gases that have polluted Earth and exacerbated global warming. However, Mars, being a cold planet, has a different problem. The temperatures on Martian surface can reach as low as –81 degrees Fahrenheit. We could use a temperature rise, which in turn releases more greenhouse gases over the years, creating a thick atmosphere that blocks most of the harmful radiation. Global warming is a problem on Earth, but on Mars, it'll be a mission. Your weakness in one environment may turn out to be a strength elsewhere.

While it is a viable option, this is expected to take a long time. One option is to place several mirrors around the Martian orbit to direct sunlight at certain spots and heat the surface. Over the years, these mirrors are expected to heat the Martian surface releasing greenhouse gases trapped in it. While this option may work slightly faster than the previous, it is still expected to take a long time.

The third option scientists are considering is a nuclear option, in which we direct ammonia-rich asteroids toward Mars using powerful nuclear-propulsion rocket engines. Eventually, these asteroids will crash into Mars, releasing ammonia and water. Ammonia raises greenhouse gas levels, might vaporize the ice, improves water levels, and would terraform Mars. These are all theoretical options at this time, and we are far from even landing on Mars, let alone living on it. But our future on Mars sounds promising. It may or may not occur in our lifetime, but the groundwork we are doing will surely lay the path to Mars for our future generations.

Floating Space Colonies

Look into the sky and imagine giant floating cities (or countries?) in the wide-open space. They may look tiny from the surface of the Earth but can be gigantic accommodating millions of people in each floating city. These cities can be modeled after the cities on the Earth. In fact, we can bring the best of multiple cities. If you have ever been to Las Vegas, imagine a floating Las Vegas in the sky, built for human habitation, instead of gambling and recreation.

But how can cities float in the space? Are these only food for sci-fi movies? This sounds like Hindu mythology where the homes of Gods float in space and could be accessed through a space vehicle. These "homes," however, do not have superpowers. They can be as real as our homes back on Earth, just more sophisticated. Let me explain this further and convince you that this is probably the best of the near-term space colonization options.

First, floating cities in space are not new. We currently have one of those "cities" floating and rotating around the Earth's orbit. It has been around since 1998. It's called the International Space Station (ISS). It's only the length of a football field, small compared to the city we want to build, but we have some precedence. City-sized ISS built for human habitation is not a problem of science but logistics and technology. We can plan the entirety of the structure beforehand and build working models and work out solutions to the problems gradually. There will be everything a human on earth needs in these floating colonies. Schools, parks, transportation systems, water, electricity, and other necessary amenities—you name it. We will have a large city with all the facilities required to lead a comfortable life. This city will have its own economy, although it can be an extension of the economy on Earth. Sounds simple? Not really.

First, the city will be orbiting the Earth in the outer space prone to lethal radiation and debris that can destroy life in an instant. Moreover, it is cut off from the direct sources of water and oxygen. We need to cover this city with a dome-like structure to protect from all the dangers. That's not an issue though because there's the technology to do that.

The problem is very low gravity in space. Moon and Mars are massive objects and hence offer certain level of gravity. Any astronaut who has spent considerable time at the ISS can tell you how life on low gravity can be. Nothing would stick to the ground. There'd be no east, west, north, and south. Bones would lose strength and muscles wouldn't flex much.

Luckily, there is a conceptual solution. This city will rotate onto itself to generate artificial gravity, a concept coined by American physicist O'Neill in his book *The High Frontier: Human Colonies in Space* in 1976, and these colonies are called O'Neill cylinders or O'Neill colonies.

O'Neill colonies can be built much closer to the Earth with the ability to reach in hours as opposed to months when compared to Mars or Moon, which takes days, with today's most advanced technologies. These colonies will make inhabitation in space possible without having to completely leave the Earth for good, that is, we can travel back and forth from Earth easily. You can have a vacation home in this colony or can live there, yet visit your relatives back on Earth as frequently as you visit your relatives on the other coast of the United States. This makes the first step into space for everyone relatively small and manageable.

However, the question is, how do we transport the materials to the space to build these gigantic cities? Do we build them on Earth, take them to space, and assemble them there? That's going to be a humongous task to lift them off of Earth's gravity. Luckily there is a concept built to address this problem.

The Moon Base

Apart from being a candidate for true human colonization, scientists believe that Moon can be our base for further reach into space, especially to build the O'Neill colonies. It's almost certain that Moon is rich in several resources, including the soil that can be used to build the O'Neill colonies and potentially as a radiation shield if we end up colonizing lunar lava tunnels. It is indeed possible to construct the O'Neill colonies on the Moon but the question is—do we need to cross-train astronauts and construction workers?

Not necessarily on a huge scale, though significant training is essential. The idea is to use advanced robots and 3D printing technologies that minimize human interference. We might have to blend the intersection of the advances in AI, robotics, and 3D printing and produce more cross-disciplinary talents. There could be temporary moon colonization just for construction workers for construction purposes. Essentially, we need space workers, but not necessarily astronauts with extensive space training and experience, as the temporary colonies will have Earth-like conditions.

Other than the abundance of natural resources, there is another major advantage of a Moon base and Moon-based construction. Moon structure can be used to build concrete. Helium can be used for fusion reactors. It's much easier to lift these off of the lunar surface than the Earth's. Remember, the Moon's gravity is one-sixth of the Earth's, which means it is six times easier to lift off a load from the lunar surface. Transporting cargo to the space can be facilitated by building a space elevator, which is essentially an elevator from the lunar surface into the space and back. That will ease the construction of the O'Neill colonies in space, much easier than building them on the Earth's surface.

But why limit with O'Neill colonies? The Moon can act as a base for radio observatories and telescopes. Moon bases sound like a promising first step into space exploration, even if the second one is something other than a floating colony.

Other "Space-Stop" Candidates

Scientists are looking at options other than Moon and Mars as our destinations, whether or not to stay there permanently. In fact, the former U.S. President Barack Obama had aimed to land on an asteroid and explore it. Some of the other candidates include Mercury that could be used for mining. Venus could be a candidate as well, although the colonies have to be floated way above its hot surface where the temperatures are similar to that of Earth. Some near-earth objects (NEO) can be moved into a safe orbit and artificially rotated for gravitation. The concept is similar to O'Neill colonies, except for the asteroid ground used instead of constructing another skeletal structure altogether.

Again, these are just a few options. There are so many moons and asteroids in our solar system that could become future candidates for space colonization. We haven't even discussed other solar systems, such as our neighboring star system Alpha Centauri and beyond.

We may not be able to settle in space in this third decade of the 21st century. It may not even happen in the fourth decade. It may, in fact, not happen in this century at all. Why should we care about all of this now? The reasons are simple. First, this will eventually happen. It's essential to understand what's coming in the space of space. Second, we are not going to flip a switch one day and decide to go settle in space. The work has to build over decades. And most importantly, all the research work that goes into space exploration will benefit the life right here on Earth.

CHAPTER 4

The BIG Future

We have seen how our society evolved from version 1.0 to today's 4.0. We have seen a flavor of the next-generation society through Falcon's tale, followed by the highlights. Now, it's time we dived into our future and analyzed how various aspects of our life are going to look like in the years to come.

Before we discuss industries, let's go through some common principles that will drive our future. Sure, various technologies, all part of the BIG—Bio, Intelligent, and Green—are shaping our future, but how are they changing our industries? What is the end result we want to achieve through these technologies? Specific challenges vary from industry to industry, hence specific goals are different, too. Goals are different for each organization within a particular industry and also are personal to each individual. But there are some common principles I believe apply to every aspect of our life. And remember, our industries are organized around our needs and support various aspects of life.

The three alphabets I believe driving our future are reduction of *work*, reduction of *worry*, and reduction of *waste* (what I call the 3Ws). Let's look at them in detail.

Work reduction is all about bringing in efficiencies through either automation, improved business processes, or both. The idea here is to optimize the work output, so more can be achieved with less effort, thus yielding more in less time. The term "work reduction" raises anxiety as it's often wrongly equated to the reduction of people. Work reduction principle doesn't, however, entail reducing work force but instead the opposite: to produce more output from the same set of resources to meet the ever-growing demand.

Worry reduction is all about ensuring the safety and well-being, both physical and mental, of everyone involved in the process. This workplace/home safety is not limited to the workers, but everyone, that includes the consumers of the products or services offered. This is also beyond the mere sense of safety, that is, avoiding other potential troubles such as legal and social.

Waste reduction is, well, all about reducing different kinds of waste. Reducing the raw material and other wastes eventually going into the landfills, however, is only one type of waste. There's another type—the wastage of effort. Often old and manual processes consume a lot of people's times, wasting a lot of effort. Lost effort is equivalent to lost productivity. If you build two plants far from each other, there is a lot of back-and-forth travel that needs to take place, resulting in energy and time wastage. Waste reduction is about saving resources where it's reasonable.

We will see how the three broad categories of technologies (BIG.) will beautifully work together to achieve these common goals, in addition to some industry and other specific goals. Again, while the specific ways differ from industry to industry, organization to organization, and individual to individual, a common approach can be defined through these three tenets: connectivity, control, and circular (the 3Cs).

Connectivity is all about uniting all the various fragmented processes, groups, and systems in an organization or our lives. The majority of the challenges any organization faces, regardless of the industry, is that the left hand doesn't know what the right hand is doing and vice versa. We face this in our daily lives as well, through various functions of our life working absolutely independently. You can take the example of different apps on your phone. They all have a brain of their own. While that may not be such a big deal for us, imagine if they all work together in a smart home through smart assistants such as Amazon Alexa, where an integrated experience is provided. However, this integration is much more than an experience for businesses and individuals; this will drive efficiencies, leading to the reduction of all 3Ws we discussed earlier.

Circularity is all about closing the loop. Part of it defines the circular economy, converting a *make-use-dispose* model into a *make-use-reuse* model, helping to reduce waste tremendously. However, there's more to it than that. An extension of one of the Cs, that is, connectivity we discussed above, makes sure the loop between various processes or the units are closed, in addition to ensuring that a connectivity is established, thus improving end-to-end communication across the organization. That will lead to better control as well. It's about having people together to accomplish more in less time instead of distributing them across various locations. "Together" can be both physical and digital.

Control is all about knowing what is happening at any given point in time at a specific business section. Through centralized control, all the connected systems can work closely together, transmitting real-time data to create a digital twin of the entire business someone can monitor on a screen. Centralized functional mapping has various applications one of which is live diagnosis of the problem in the system. For instance, if an equipment is about to go bad, the sensor detects that and the same is marked in red on the digital twin. But it gets even better. There is no need to closely monitor the process. An alert will be sent to the person in charge; a service order is automatically created for the repair; and any replaceable parts are automatically ordered. By that, we not only ensured the continuity of business, but also avoided work hazards. However, control doesn't only entail regularity on a technical level. It is also about your dominance in finances, assets, health, safety, and marketing, among others, through increased predictability and reduced surprises. The same applies to our life as well.

With this brief introduction, let's dive right into our BIG future, peeling one layer at a time. To be able to give a more predictable view of the future, I will hop back to past occasionally and try to put concepts into perspective. That's because the future is never complete without the understanding of the past.

Future of Food (Agriculture)

Agriculture is the oldest industry known to humankind and still is the chief source of food production. It was a means to both sustenance and currency. It will be crucial to review some of the trends in this critical industry and, most importantly, how agriculture is going to look in the future.

Agriculture is a general term used for raw food production and can broadly be divided into three groups on the basis of the products they yield. First is "vegan" culture products, meaning agriculture of plant-based food such as grains, fruits, and vegetables. The second is animal culture products, agriculture of animal-based food such as meat and milk. And the third is aquaculture and relates to water-based food such as fish and shrimp. To make things simpler, I will use the words farming and agriculture interchangeably.

The Society 1.0 ancestors depended more on on-demand or impromptu farming. The mode of food production was daily gathering: hunting animals or picking fruits and vegetables for a certain time during the day, often just enough to feed the family for a day. The rest of the day was spent in leisure, doing whatever they liked, whether it's sleeping, "socializing," or simply relaxing. This "work–life balance" model was acceptable, given that global population, especially its density, was not huge. For example, the upper estimate of world population as of 10000 BC was 10 million, according to census.gov (2021). That means we had one person for every 20 square miles back in the day, leaving plenty of food resources for everyone. If we take the lower population estimation of one million total global population, it gives approximately 200 square miles of land for every live person. As the population grew, food became scarce and hunting and gathering had to become more common, for longer hours during the day, adding up to a choking point of high demand. Without wonder, the necessity was met by the exploding agricultural revolution.

Then, the concept of farming developed in Society 2.0 to improve the predictability of available food. Lands were prepared for farming; societies grew around those lands. With this evolution, our ancestors could "mass-produce" food in an organized manner and distribute and store it for near-future adversities. However, they still depended highly on direct natural food sources, which were hinged on nature's unpredictability or even hostility. At times of harsh weather or high competition, no food was available. Often, the entire batch of foods was infested by insects; the people went hungry for sustained periods of time due to this. This food scarcity was rather more prominent and depressive when the infestation was more widespread due to undiscovered bacteria and viruses. Not just plants, animals were also infected. Birds, insects, and animals acted as nature's intruders and the best solution we had back in the day to protect farms from these intruders was a scarecrow, outside of manual guarding, of course. Long days of manual labor and being at the mercy of nature were the two extremes the farming people had to endure.

Everything began to transform and evolve with the industrial revolution in Society 3.0, and agriculture was not any different. Tractors and other farming equipment reduced manual labor and improved efficiencies. Fertilizers improved production. Pesticides helped beat insects and other intruders. Advances in the medical field helped cure animal infections. Gene editing made plants, animals, and birds stronger and better, including the production of "pseudo-natural," brand-new, food types borne out of advancing technologies.

Fast forward to the information society, Society 4.0; the transformative technologies continue to improve, making farming easier and better. The access to the data from the entire food supply chain spectrum has enabled information technology to bring about revolution in crop planning, production, and distribution, by streamlining processes. Demand is forecasted more accurately, and so is production, so the supply can better match the demand. Thanks to all the computing power that was developed in the last few decades, distribution networks are streamlined and the crops are tracked from their departure from the farm until they end up on the market shelves. Satellites help us better understand weather patterns and reduce the nature's menace to farms and farmers—good news that the latter can get advanced notice for natural calamities. Manual and animal labor are replaced by machines, streamlining planning to plowing, and picking to packing. Advances in biotech continue to bring more food options as well. This is how humans eat today.

However, we are at an inflection point. The agricultural industry is facing numerous challenges. First, the agriculture sector has ended up being one of the biggest emitters of carbon dioxide, the greenhouse gas (GHG) responsible for climate change. Together with forestry and other land use, agriculture is responsible for just under 25 percent of all human-created GHG emissions, according to the climate reality project. The agricultural industry is challenged to go "green" yet produce all the nutritious food we all demand.

With global population on the rise, the one thing everyone will need is food to survive. The production capacity, hence, must continue to increase to meet the demand. In order to meet the other basic necessity of this growing population such as shelter, agricultural lands are being converted to residential places, leaving less land to produce more food. Climate changing rapidly has been directly impacting this grand old industry. Consumers of food are becoming smarter through increased exposure to information, putting pressure on farmers to meet consumers' tastes and expectations. The young generation is moving away from agriculture toward other "cooler" industries. Despite advances in information technology, food continues to get wasted, with an estimated 133 billion pounds worth $161.6 billion being dumped every year in the United States alone, according to a U.S. Department of Agriculture report (Buzby, Wells, and Hyman 2014).

These are just some of the key challenges the agriculture industry is facing today. So, what is the solution? What is the future of agriculture and how will it overcome the above challenges? Here is my top list.

Regenerative Farming

Dubbed as the "future of farming," regenerative farming is a broad term focusing on using and enriching natural resources instead of destroying and depleting them. While the specifics vary from place to place, to customize methods to locally available resources, fundamentally, regenerative farming revolves around a few principles.

The first principle is *do not mess with the land*. As idealistic as it sounds, merely tilling the land is the largest contributor to GHG emissions. It also kills the important microbes in the soil required for nourishment. The second principle is *use the natural ecosystem to feed each other*: grow a variety of crops that help each other's productivity, including a combination of plants and animals. Growing winter-friendly crops in between harvests to protect the soil to increase its nutrients is an example. Converting unused produce and animal wastes into compost and adding it back to the soil is another example. Similarly, the third is *crop rotation*, which is an extension of the second principle. Crop rotation alternates the plantation of one crop with the other often to improve the productivity of the soil. Likewise, the fourth principle is *go natural*. Going natural rests on the principle of minimal intervention. Protect crops and minimize the use of chemicals or any other unnecessary intervention, gradually tapering toward null.

Essentially, regenerative farming uses natural techniques but uses them intelligently to maximize production. How can a farmer decide which crops to grow together and how to rotate crops? That's where AI comes in. I see regenerative farming as a beautiful merger of preindustrial natural farming techniques and 21st-century information technology.

If you are into farming, make sure you embrace regenerative farming techniques. It's not just a cool method to practice, it's the right method and, most importantly, this method gives you the best financial returns. I wouldn't invest in an agricultural business that doesn't currently employ this method or has plans to do so in the future.

Computer Vision Replacing Scarecrows and Technology Safeguarding the Farms

I grew up around a lot of farms. My favorite was a nearby mango farm, which we as kids would visit occasionally, to pluck a mango or two when we wanted to be mischievous (which was always). An old man—I still remember his face, it was scary—managed and guarded the farm. He made frequent visits to the farm, keeping stray animals and kids away and was functionally against our mission—which was to ensure we don't get caught. Although the old man did a great job at making these rounds, we would be successful in nearly two-thirds of all our attempts.

Today, the surveillance cameras replace the old guard, whether fixed in several locations or constantly tracking on a mobile robot. Computer vision processes these images and acts whenever it detects anything unusual. In the case of mischievous kids, perhaps an announcement that it is watching us would have been sufficient. At best, computer vision can summon a drone to chase away the birds or even call the cops in case it detects something more serious. It can also single out inactive animals in the case of an animal farm to detect diseases and take preventive actions before they spread.

Aerial Drones

Imagine the same scenario as above, but the eyes in the air this time, instead of fixed cameras, or on a mobile robot. The drone video is processed by advanced AI-based computer vision to detect not only external intruders but also pests, insects, and intruders that humans can hardly detect. Drones can also be used to plant seeds where digging is not required, spraying pesticides, dropping fertilizers, and even to water any plants in tough-to-reach places.

Smart Fabric and Accessories Protecting Animal Farms

Smart watches aren't just for humans. Smart collars, bands, and other accessories will detect livestock activities and vital signs and get processed almost on a real-time basis, complementing the data received and processed by computer vision. In case any particular animal on the farm is less active than usual, or any animal develops a temperature, it can be isolated and treated before the disease spreads, saving a lot of lives.

Robotic Friends Dominating Agriculture

Autonomous tractors, autonomous seed planting robotic helpers, pesticide and fertilizer spraying bots, watering bots, fruit and vegetable picking bots, animal showering bots, animal feeding bots, meat slaughtering bots, meat sorting bots, packing bots—these are just a handful of smart bots that will dominate our farms. However, it doesn't mean robots will be able to outgrow humans or rather outgrow crop production.

Revamping Local Farming

Farming was localized for a long time. Thanks to the continued industrial revolution and globalization, food production is being limited to a few designated lands and is being distributed across the globe with chains of intricate supply-and-demand architectures. I still remember the exciting story someone from Sweden told me when they had a first-in-their-lifetime experience of tasting a banana arriving from South America.

So much for the merits of the global agro-industry. The global transport of goods, as much as it feeds the world, also contributes to global warming. Moreover, it's not the same as freshly picked produce. Well-informed consumers demand food that is both fresh and healthy for the environment. And the only way to craft this combination is through forced local farming. The good news is that advances in technology can now mimic climatic conditions required for crops anywhere in the world. This is the future of farming. And this concept might democratize and decentralize farming, growing the number of farmers nurturing food in their backyards and providing to the community. You do not require big enough backyard for this form of farming because you can rent a container and convert it into an indoor farm. Why not turn your farming passion and your free time into an income-generating business? You can start small without deploying any fancy technology or tools and work your way up. However, make sure you employ regenerative farming techniques.

Catering to Both GMO and Non-GMO Consumers

Thanks to all the progress in genetic engineering, genetically modified (GM) foods have been hitting our shelves almost since the last three decades. An example of this is a nutrition-rich rice. Genetic engineering will continue to produce more nutritious food and increase food production. Of many GM-tech's pick points, one of them is that foods can be modified to suit the environment or make it friendly. However, there's also another side to this story. Many people are skeptical of GM foods because they think they don't know enough of this domain, of the environmental, health, and nutritional repercussions. Irrespective of the science behind it, the debate will continue, hence the need for continued production of genetically unmodified food is inevitable.

3D Farming—Farming More in Less

We think of farms as large pieces of open lands filled with plants, trees, or animals or large sources of water. These farms are 2D. With reduced land space in general and the push to grow crops locally, indoor farming is growing in popularity these days. How do you make the most out of the limited indoor space? Also known as vertical farming, this method turns farming area into a three-dimensional structure. It simply means, in addition to using length and breadth of the land, the height should also be employed in farming, which is similar to vertical urbanization, out of similar concerns. Stack the crop on top of each other in layers in an indoor, controlled environment and that way we can decrease the space needed for farming. More to it, indoor 3D farming allows the climate to be strictly controlled and without the dangers of nature's wrath.

3D Printing—Print Everything on Demand

Day-to-day tools, indoor farming structures, pots, neck collars, feeding tools, and even helper robots—you can print everything on the farm, on demand. There is no need to spend days, if not weeks or months, shopping around, purchasing, and then transporting to the farm. Because of the possibility of extreme customization in the case of 3D custom printing the tools, effort put into designing the tools won't go waste because the exact specifications are always met.

Organic Farming

In the old days, agriculture used to be purely organic. This was as soon as and even after many years since farming started. Gradually, the need for upping the production was felt owing to increased population and thus came fertilizers, chemicals, insecticides, pesticides, rodenticides, and all the imaginable -cides we can think of: terminators of the unwanted that "harm" our crops.

This went on only till we realized chemical-borne foods harmed humans and environment and we were in a constant juggle of balancing the increase in productivity with health hazards. Because of decades of apprehension, the demand for chemical-free food is growing by the day and well-informed consumers have been opting for "genuine" organic products. We will soon go back to being 100 percent organic if we can tackle the demand–supply gap and meet the production capacity.

But growing organic food is challenging. For example, to be considered 100 percent organic, the poultry must be raised steroids- and chemicals-free, and every component of the food they eat must be organic. The bigger challenge will be to prove that it's 100 percent organic. This is where blockchain tracking can come in, which can certify and verify the full life cycle of the produce, from farm to the kitchen table. That provides complete peace of mind to the consumers who want to go fully organic. Nevertheless, this technology may not have a big-bang adoption, especially in the beginning. But with time, if one company joins such certification, the rest may follow suit. If not, they risk disruption. If you had a choice between one organic product certified by blockchain, slightly costlier, and another one uncertified but inexpensive, which one would you choose?

IoT Bringing It All Together

Technologies can seamlessly work together to form an integrated and coordinated farm. This may include moisture sensors triggering the sprinkler system, heat sensors spraying mist or pulling the screen down to provide shade, computer vision summoning the drone or calling the cops, temperature sensor alerting the farmer of a sick animal, plowing and seed-planting robot working together, plucking robot updating the stock levels in the backend enterprise resource planning (ERP) system, and a whole lot of other applications. The Internet of things (IoT) will form a digital ecosystem of all the various tools and components involved in the end-to-end farming ecosystem to provide an integrated experience to the farmer.

Advanced AI for Real-Time Farming Insights

As we've already discussed, data are the next big thing in all the domains. Right information at the right time is what helps farmers make better decisions. Granted that it is not an easy task. The information from these different sources must be processed with huge computing power, analyzed, and the concerned people in the loop must be alerted, eliminating false alarms, for this to work. For example, the temperature coming from the wearable sensor on the animal alone cannot be used to alert the farmer that the animal is sick. Compare that with the data coming from other animals, factor in outside temperature, look into the animal's history and contact with the outside life—all before the alarm bells are pressed. There is a need to analyze past patterns and other criteria and precisely tell the farmer when to plant the seeds to maximize the outcome. Process the data being received from all the sensors and factor in historical data and data available on the Internet to predict risks before they become issues, such as a pest attack. However, the Internet is full of information, and only certain sources can be trusted. Spotting these sources is, too, not an easy task. The need for a supersmart digital bot to achieve all this is dire. Only advanced AI can devour information of this magnitude, learn from it over time, and work independently of humans. Only then the farmers and their workers can focus on what they do best—farming.

In summary, the future of farming is going to look a lot different. We will see a beautiful merger of the sciences of farming, which in themselves are evolving rapidly, including more natural, advanced, and organic techniques, making farming one of the coolest skills to possess in the future.

Future of Shelter (and Construction)

Shelter undoubtedly falls right after food on the priority when it comes to listing our necessities. Let's review the past trends, current challenges, and the future of this most crucial need. First, however, let's expand our conversation to the construction industry in general, covering infrastructure in addition to shelter.

Our great ancestors looked to natural houses such as trees and caves for shelter in the early part of Society 1.0, thus the name "cavemen" (or cavewomen). These people figured ways to shelter their families using stones and tree branches toward the end of Society 1.0, thus giving rise to first primitive concept of homes.

Fast forward to Society 2.0, the agriculture society; this is where the emphasis on shelter skyrocketed with the formation of societies around the farmlands. While construction techniques evolved over time, it was predominantly through natural resources such as clay, stones, and wood that homes were built with. The construction methods varied with civilizations owing to developing techniques, needs, and resource availability. For example, in ancient China, people would use a lot of wood for construction due to its abundance and faster time to value. Ancient Greeks used a combination of stone, clay, and mud bricks to build beautiful structures. And ancient Romans used concrete, made by mixing lime and volcanic rock.

The raised standards of Society 3.0 gave rise to new construction methods with the invention of Portland cement that industrialized building with the help of bricks, nails, and other tools. Steel went into mass production and formed an integral part of high-rise buildings. Black asphalt topped the roads and reduced the work done during transportation. Dynamite helped dig tunnels and, with various advancements together, structured bridges. Automation slowly took over manual and time-consuming tasks through powerful machines that can work faster than humans. However, the build boom was only limited to industrialized societies with a majority of the world still using the construction techniques of the previous society, mostly due to the unavailability of resources, both money and raw materials.

While the construction methods continued to improve, the information society, Society 4.0, brought along several other transformations to the construction industry through digitization of its various aspects. Take, for instance, better visibility in the movement of raw materials. This not only expanded raw material transportation around the globe, but also provided better control on the supply chain. Construction design got digitized through computer-based 3D models. The entire construction process can now be better managed using project management tools. Work is scheduled and tracked digitally, together with worker's productivity. Control on finances has improved through more efficient IT systems supporting the financial backbone. Buildings that can withstand deadlier natural calamities such as earthquakes were built with more sophistication and design.

However, the question is whether all these advances in the information technology are doing everything needed to bolster the construction sector. Lately, construction industry is facing a number of challenges. First and foremost is building stronger and higher-lifespan structures that not only withstand the nature's wrath, but are also eco-efficient. This is where design innovations come in as the success of any construction lies in the quality of its design. Design errors still cause construction owners, whether individuals or companies, to lose a lot of investments and lives. Construction is an investment-rich business with lurking market risks only waiting a step ahead. A market crash at the end is going to throw all the investment down the drain. Potential issues to supply chain must be considered, minimizing any material shortages. Furthermore, fluctuation of raw material costs and missed deadlines further aggravate the risks of uncertainties. So, forecasting cost balances considering market trends is crucial in reducing market risks. There are several other factors such as weather and regulations that impact construction projects. On top of that, safety of construction workers is also key. Unsafe construction practices cause millions of dollars damage to construction companies and may put brand and reputation at stake—maintaining which is very essential in this business. Not the least, intrabusiness disruptions and employee dissatisfaction also form one of the major hurdles. It is safe to say that information technology isn't doing as much as it should in alleviating the wounds of the construction business.

What lies ahead for the construction sector vis-à-vis the use of technology that further addresses the unaddressed problems? Here is the beginning of key trends toward novel construction frontiers.

Advanced AI Will Plan and Design Better Construction Projects

We currently have multiple software solutions that design construction projects—be it housing, roads, dams, or tunnels. The only intervention needed to take that first step toward construction intelligence is making the design solutions intelligent. These AI-based design tools will only use publicly available data to design smart buildings. The AI's learning algorithm will read the available regulations, energy-efficient techniques, and methods to fireproof and earthquake-proof, among others, to design a safe building. Various levels of customization will be available, for instance, using green technologies. The AI will learn the methodologies to turning processes and structures green giving you a green house (not to be confused with greenhouse). Of course, you will be able to feed the AI with the sources you want it to use. It will read market trends and give you a timeframe for your project, depending on market forecasts. The software might also consider market trends and can offer you less risky material options. Workers will be more looked after and will be safer in their workspaces. All you need to do is ensure you follow the plan. This AI will learn over time from errors it makes and get smarter, for example, using past precedents such as minor mistakes in designing structures and preventing future errors in the next designs. That's why in the initial learning period of the machine, it's common for a human expert to check flaws in the designs. The good thing is the more the machine gets to design, the better it will get.

However, beyond the current set of challenges, we are undoubtedly entering a brand-new era in construction for both housing and general infrastructure. Here are the other major areas of transformation in the construction industry.

Smart Homes

"Alexa, set downstairs thermostat to 72." "Siri, turn off the fountain." "Alexa, play my favorite playlist on Piano." Today's homes are filled with smart assistants that respond to and act on commands like this. Several homes are already filled with smart appliances, smart gadgets, and even smart furniture. More "things" will become smart as technology matures. Is this what I am referring to when I say smart home? Not exactly. Look at this as a basic level of home automation. We have discussed under Chapter 3 how our world will soon be dominated by AI with AI predicted to be here, there, and everywhere. Every aspect of your home will be smart and connected, including your toilet. However, most importantly, every smart "thing" in the future has to get smarter over time through learning from the data it collects (and other devices it connects). We have covered these topics under highlights in the previous chapter. Only thing I can assure you though is our homes will continue to get smarter and if you are in the smart home business, you are in it to win it.

Brick Batteries

We know that future is all about moving away from fossil fuels and toward renewable energy. And one of the perpetual sources of renewable energy, at least for five billion more years, is solar energy. Your home is probably powered by solar panels at the moment. But why have a roof and place panels on top? Why not merge the two? Solar power-generating roofing tiles don't just act as protecting tiles but also as a medium for tapping enormous energy. You can have your entire roof filled with solar tiles or a portion.

But tiles only convert light into electricity. It's the battery packs where the energy is stored. One of the disadvantages of this battery pack energy storage system is you need a considerable space to keep the inverters and batteries at home. The more your home demands energy, the larger your battery. There's probably a solution. With smart homes comes smart walls. If you remember Falcon's story, the entire energy Falcon's home generates was stored in the walls. What if you get to store the power generated by your roof in none other than your wall, too? The age-old bricks made of clay are the perfect-strength porous devices that scientists are interested in to store electricity. Pumping certain gases through the bricks to facilitate chemical reactions with its components can turn regular bricks into capacitors—devices like batteries but that supply energy instantly. These bricks are already into development: "Regular bricks can be transformed into energy storage devices," as reported by CNN digital (Kann 2020). While there's much to be done to materialize this concept, initial research looks promising. It may not be long before the roof generates the renewable energy during the day and the bricks store them for use at night.

Go Green

A "green" house (different from *greenhouse* which traps solar rays and maintains a higher temperature inside than outside) helps address the effects of climate change, a significant crisis planet Earth is facing. Of course, moving to renewable energy such as solar is part of the plan. However, it's more than that. Expanding our smart home discussion further, imagine fitting your home with smart windows. These windows can block the sun's rays when it's hot and allow them to enter when it's cold, to limit electricity usage. That would amount to a whole lot of energy conservation. Imagine if all the waste and rainwater collected from households gets stored and recycled for nonpotable uses? And use of wind energy, natural light, and energy-efficient appliances was promoted? All of these start with energy-efficient design, using advanced AI-based design tools. The goal for all future homes is net-zero emission, which simply means your net contribution to GHGs must be zero, and you do that by taking measures to remove the same amount of gases you are adding to the environment.

Charging Stations

The march toward electric vehicles is eminent. Who hasn't heard of the tremendous transformation in the auto industry brought in by Tesla, leading to its exponential growth? All trends indicate that most gas stations will go out of business in the future, if not all of them, replaced by charging stations, especially ones alongside freeways, catering to long-distance travelers. Note that many local gas stations will eventually run out of business because people charge their cars at home and stores. Moreover, battery technology is developing at such a fast pace that the frequency of charges will come down as well. The change will not be sudden and total. Electric vehicles will start to replace gasoline- and diesel-based cars slowly but steadily within the next few decades, starting with new cars coming into the market. Will gasoline car industries completely disappear? Probably not. Many will simply hang on to their combustion engine cars for longer than they should, leaving a fragmented ecosystem around such cars. There will always be demand for some vintage cars, too, but they will be a minority on our roadways in a few decades.

With limited use of gas stations, what will be the future of those convenience stores next to them? Will that disappear, too? I believe they will evolve into entertainment centers to amuse families who stop by to reload their cars.

Charging Roads

With the growth of electric and autonomous car, future roads must be friendly to these robots. First, roadways around the globe will slowly be upgraded to meet the needs of autonomous cars. For example, the lane dividers will be clear and will contain symbols autonomous cars can understand, potentially with the ability to directly connect with future cars as well. Traffic lights, stop signs, curvy roads—all of them will be robot-friendly. But the most exciting feature of the future roads will be the ability to charge your car while driving. No, they'll not be wired like electric trains, if you're imagining an electric cable constantly connected to your car from underneath. It will be inductive charging, what's commonly known as wireless charging. Your car drives itself, while the road charges it. All you need to do is sit and relax. While Falcon drove back to his home, the road charged his car.

Spaceports

The first port we built was a seaport to cater to all the marine traffic. Then came along "bus ports" (stations), "train ports," and eventually airports. We have seen how airports have been transforming in the last century, growing into "experience centers" and "shopping hubs" from simple transportation points. The next port humans are striving to build is not so ubiquitous yet but aiming to be in future. It's the spaceport that lets you travel from one part of our world to another in minutes zipping through space in a spacecraft instead of flying inside the atmosphere in an airplane.

E-Mailed Homes

Homes are generally meant to be fixed structures, built with a lot of energy over long periods of time. But there are also manufactured homes that are built in a factory and shipped. But how about homes that can be e-mailed, designed by a designer up to the last detail using an advanced AI? You simply "print" it at your home or rather a construction site using a giant 3D printer. Large-structure 3D printing is already nearly ubiquitous. It's getting inexpensive, too. That is available in 2022 and the technology will only become cheaper and more efficient in the future. A *Forbes* news from April 2021 states: "3D-Printed California Community Shows the Technology's Huge Potential for Home Construction" (Castenson 2021) or from *The Guardian*, the same month: "Dutch Couple Become Europe's First Inhabitants of a 3D-Printed House" (Boffey 2021). Homes and other structures printed by these giant robots are the future of construction, especially as we are beginning to conquer other planets where it's much easier to send a giant robotic 3D printer instead of masons-turned-astronauts.

But will 3D printing dominate the construction industry here on earth? The answer is a resounding yes. Even if the entire house is not

3D printed, major portions of the house will be. Custom homes and other structures will always have a place, although parts of them will be 3D printed. 3D printing technology is here to stay and construction industry is no exception.

Great Suburban Expansion

Our civilization predominantly centered in one location in the past, called city centers or downtown areas. Back then, we only had urban and rural areas. Urban areas began expanding into suburban areas, also known as suburbs, creating a brand-new layer in between urban and rural. The emergence of this liminal space has proliferated toward the beginning of the information society: more people moved away from city centers into these suburbs and settled there for good. As of 2020 to 2022, this trend has accelerated as several companies allowed their employees to work from home following the COVID-19 protocols. The question is, will this trend continue?

While this may slow down, I believe suburb expansion started way before COVID and it is here to stay. This will partly be supported by companies themselves continuing to move out of city centers not just to reduce costs, but also to hunt talent that is itself moving into suburbs. Moreover, concentrated civilization is simply not a sustainable model considering the population drive in the major cities.

Undoubtedly, we will see increased construction activity in the future, mostly driven by the growing demand of an increasing population. The United States will also see significant improvements in its infrastructure, thanks to the $1 trillion bipartisan infrastructure bill Congress signed into law in November 2021 (Pramuk 2021). This "turn inward" gesture may cause a ripple effect and push other countries to upgrade their infra-structures as well. Growing demand will lead to more innovation and automation. Construction industry will grow smarter by the day and green technologies such as renewables, EV, and net neutrality will be the major driving forces. Whether you own a piece of construction to settle in, have a real estate as an active investment, are an entrepreneur in this field, or are simply a passive investor, following these trends will give you the best value to your buck.

Future of Clothing and Accessories

Another human necessity alongside food and shelter is clothing. From covering themselves with leaves and other natural materials to the invention of fabric, clothing has not only been tied to human evolution, but also carries a rich history. It's unknown why exactly our ancestors started using clothes but there are two major theories and both could be true at the same time. First, clothing and accessories have been used to attract the opposite sex. Ancient humans used body marks, tattoos, and other forms of body art in addition to attractive natural clothing. Second, humans are warm-blooded animals and it's difficult to maintain that warmth without a thick coat of fur on the outside as our skin is not as tough as other animals to withstand extreme weathers. With climatic changes, the need to add artificial layers and hence stop the body from losing heat grew. Migration from Africa to settle in other parts of the world cemented the need to cover bodies further because of exposure to harsher weather conditions. But there must be other reasons behind.

Society 1.0 started with clothes made of leaves, animal skin, and other naturally available material. Humans realized that raw natural clothing dried and decomposed and didn't last longer. Moreover, they were less comfortable, did not preserve much heat, and attracted herbivorous animals than warding them off. This gave an impetus to the discovery of fabric. The primitive fabric-making machinery produced variations of linen, wool, and silk. Slowly, as civilizations advanced into Society 2.0, fashion became symbolic to each civilization. Each civilization represented a rich history of clothing styles and use of certain accessories and jewelry. Such traditional clothing can still be seen in various parts of the world, tied to various civilizations.

The invention of a spinning and weaving machine revolutionized clothing, automating the long and laborious task of manual weaving. This marked the beginning of the great industrial revolution, leading to Society 3.0 that evolved over time to the present-day great society you and I live in. Clothing played such a vital role in peoples' lives that people used it for displaying ostentatious status symbols to making political statements. More automation came along in the textile world and led to larger-scale production of clothes in shorter timeframes, making clothing more affordable and reachable to everyone. But the true revolution in clothing and accessories can only be owed to the creation of artificial or synthetic fibers such as polyester, nylon, and rayon. This enabled clothing to be dyed in a plethora of colors, made them more durable, cheaper, and also more accessible in the latter parts of Society 3.0.

The information society, Society 4.0, brought in better visibility and efficiency to the end-to-end supply chain, giving clothing manufacturers the ability to better forecast demand to meet the supply. Efficiencies in supply chain made "fast fashion" possible; what it meant to the consumers was fashion was no longer tied to durability. This trend was pioneered by companies such as Zara, H&M, and Forever 21, which, instead of mass producing the same clothes over and over, started a new business model wherein they changed their fashion trends every season, sometimes even multiple times a season. Manufacturing optimization, globalization, and invention of synthetic fabrics helped them deliver clothes to the consumers at a lower cost, appealing them to buy more each time, or as often as they change their designs. When I compare this to the mere one set of new clothes I got per year as a kid to the present-day kids who rarely appear in the same clothes twice in family functions, I cannot help but pity myself.

Clothing industry is at an inflection point today, similar to most other industries that are going through an enormous transformation. We will come to changing trends shortly, but at first it should be acknowledged that the industry is facing numerous challenges. Fashion industry is the second largest polluter in the world, standing right next to the oil industry. Resources and chemicals required to grow and store raw materials (e.g., cotton) and synthetics, such as polyester, have deemed the entire industry almost nonbiodegradable. And we haven't even started talking about all the animals we kill for leather and all the GHGs that emit during the transportation of garments across the globe, among other things. Fashion industry is a nightmare to environmentalism.

Although the entire supply chain process has improved drastically during the information era, waste is still a major factor in this industry. Waste equals lost money, burden on our planet Earth, or both. Fake products are another issue primarily impacting high-end brands. You and I are well informed today compared to our forefathers and foremothers.

We demand better fashion, responsible fashion to be precise, and less wastage. Ways of shopping have now changed, moving from in-store visits to at-home clicks. On top of everything, technology is simply overtaking the clothing industry. How do we address these challenges and keep up with drastic changes our technologies and societies are going through? These are the key trends in clothing which I believe deserve attention:

Computing Fabric

While reviewing how AI is going to dominate our lives, we briefly touched on the concept of smart fabric. All outfits we wear: t-shirts, shirts, pants, hats, shoes, jewelry, blankets, towels, and even underwear will go smart in the future, offering some level of computation through inserted technology. T-shirts monitoring vital signs sending your wellness data to your doctor, location-tracking jackets helping to rescue missing people, dirt-sensing carpets auto summoning the vacuum cleaner, temperature-sensing pants auto adjusting the heat, heat-sensing window curtains auto regulating themselves and even adjusting the thermostat, and sleep-monitoring bed sheets sending wellness tips to your inbox: these are some of the potential use cases for smart fabric. Smart textile industry will be worth $5.4 billion by 2025 with a compound annual growth rate (CAGR) of 30.4 percent from 2019 to 2025, according to Grand View Research (2019). If you remember the attendant back in Falcon's story, you'd realize that not just the t-shirt, but the doctor your t-shirt is interacting with is also a tech. With a growing number of companies working on intelligent clothing, who knows what clothes you wear have to offer in near future.

Smart Fashion Designers

Paying millions of dollars to fashion designers will become a thing of the past. AI will design clothes much better than humans. Fashion designing is a complex business. A new design must follow the trends and appeal to specific age groups. Who is better at following trends and understanding people's pulse than Mr. I—the Internet? AI will scan through social media, follow market trends, innovate and experiment within the designs, and come up with styles appealing to a specific audience, improving the chances of faster sales. But that's not all. AI will forecast demands based on these data and match the item's production, reducing overall waste.

At-Home Trial Rooms

Tired of going to a store and standing in the line to try out clothes? How about bringing that trial room to your home instead? Select the garment you like and augmented reality (AR) will not only tell you the exact size you need, but also will show you how exactly you look with that on you. Immersion technologies will create an alternate virtual world centered on you. Do you want to see yourself with that dress on at a wedding? Your virtual trial room can create that experience for you. These at-home trial rooms will be much better than the physical trial rooms. That's because you can try as many sets of clothes for as many situations.

Closet Tailor

How often do you get up in the morning not knowing what to wear and simply cycle through all those clothes? Your smart mirror in your smart closet will learn your schedule, read the weather information from the Internet, get your "mood data" from your smart watch or blanket, read your past clothing patterns, and will tell you what you should wear. However, there could be more. If you don't have what your closet recommends for you, you can simply 3D print the outfit it designed. All you need to do is to put the outfit on and smile. This technology is not very distant.

Goodbye Synthetic

As we discussed earlier, clothing industry is the second-most polluter partly due to the nonbiodegradable nature of synthetic fabric. A piece of polyester in the ocean either ends up being in the ocean for hundreds of years or inside an aquatic animal. The same animal then might make its way to your dinner plate. On that note, clothing manufacturers already are feeling an obligation to move toward green clothing. Add potential regulations on top, and most importantly the reluctance of informed customers like you and I, chemical-based fabric's future in clothing doesn't seem so bright. That said, consumers need to be wary of more and more companies taking their aggressive "green" agendas to the media in an attempt to look environmentally conscious—which turns out to be nothing but politically correct marketing gimmicks splashing a tint of greenwash. However, there are always those who want to make a change. And being in that change now will definitely pay later on.

Leather in a Lab

The history of animal cruelty is as old as human civilization. Animal rights organization *People for the Ethical Treatment of Animals* (PETA) quotes FAO data in which it states that each year, we slaughter more than a billion animals ("Leather" 2022). In another article by PETA, it states how shocking animal killing has been: "Roughly 3,000 silkworms are killed to make a single pound of silk. That means that billions, if not trillions, of them are killed every year" (Toliver 2018).

Humans love leather and silk. Though they're achieved by immoral means, there's no way humans have been able to dump them altogether. How can we stop animal cruelty and continue to wear things we like? The solution, however, has been there since the mid-1880s. Synthetic look-alikes, such as Rayon, invented in 1884 did the job, but then in the wake of environmental disasters, we felt synthetic had to go sooner or later no matter what. Scientists are working on creating leather- and silk-like materials through advanced biotechnology, a concept called bio-mimicry, mimicking natural characteristics of these animals and worms. Call it "leather in a lab" or "silk in a test tube." These will not only look like leather and silk, but feel and behave like them, with biodegradability, because they are produced using advanced biotechnology.

Authenticity Tracking

Imagine buying a gently used Louis Vuitton purse you always liked through someone you met on Facebook. A month later, you realize it was fake. There are thousands of people who're tricked into buying counterfeit goods of reputed names and none who're doing enough to curb the situation. Today, counterfeit goods have become one of the biggest challenges high-end consumer brands face. Counterfeit industry is estimated at over $1.2 trillion, $450 billion of which is valued to be tied to the fashion industry alone. Manufacturers have been attempting to prove authenticity using various methods such as assignment of serial numbers, but every year they're outsmarted by cunning comebacks from these fake products.

But this may change. Blockchain technology can become one of the most suitable methods to track products from their birth to consumption and degradation. You will be able to trace the product's entire life to know whether it's authentic or not. But this is not a tracking device and it will not invade anyone's privacy. How it works is pretty simple. Imagine registering and maintaining every high-end product through a smart tag such as a QR code in a "distributed ledger," managed by multiple agents around the globe, that not only tracks the origin of every product, but its entire supply chain process. An authorized user can know the product's full history simply by accessing this blockchain. Any manipulation, in an attempt to tamper, must be done in multiple places through the blockchain, thus not only making it difficult but practically impossible to manipulate the products' authenticity.

Recycling

Recycling is another trend that is picking up in the clothing and fashion industry. More retailers, especially fast fashion companies, are promising this, given sustainability goals. However, this is easier said than done. True recycling means reusing the fabric to make new sets of clothes and is only possible when clothes are not made of synthetic raw material. Else, recycling is difficult to the point it becomes almost impossible. That's why I believe jury is still out on that promise, unless the original fabric is made of recyclable material. However, a definite trend to watch out for is resale of used clothes. More retailers are jumping onto this bandwagon of preowned clothes that is projected as cool. This trend has already picked up steam for luxury clothes and accessories. Big names such as Lululemon have also begun their journeys down this road. *CNBC* reported: "Lululemon is testing a resale program where shoppers can sell and buy used items" (Thomas 2021). This makes sense because this is a win-win-win-win model, meaning it's good for the planet, it helps you make money off your gently used clothes, new owners can buy them cheap, and companies can resell them for a profit. Watch this space.

These were some of the key futuristic trends in the clothing industry. It's certain that I didn't cover all of them, but these will give you an idea of where the future of clothing is headed. The summary is not only that technology will be more heavily employed in the clothing industry, but it is also that clothing will become technology: either through smart fabrics built on high technology or fabrics made in a lab using biotechnology.

With all of this going on, what will happen to the fashion industry's designing jobs in the future? Provided that the ones with "taste" will still look for personalized assistance—like the book lovers who oppose digital readers—fashion designers and personal clothing advisors will not be entirely gone. They will just be less in number but will surely turn to AI for help.

Future of Money (Financial Services)

Money is simply an entity that determines how you live in this world: what you eat, where you live, what you wear, what you drive, where your kids go to school, and so on. Though it does not define your state of mind or intellectuality, it defines rich and poor and determines the quality of everyone's life. Let's spend some time understanding its history and pondering its future.

It's a given that though you attracting money depends on hard work and situational favorability, there's a good chance you and money will get along if you mold every principle of earning money into a skill. To do that, it becomes necessary to understand what and how money is. Below is the history of the financial services industry or, loosely, the history of money.

Early Trading: The Barter System

As with all other industries, the journey starts in Society 1.0. Money as a concept never existed in the hunter-gatherer society. How did they buy things then? The answer is they didn't. Instead, they bartered things in exchange for goods and services.

Let's say John hunted two deer and his friend Rob collected 30 apples. John shares one deer with Rob in exchange for 15 apples. The value of those goods was directly negotiated by the parties involved. This point-to-point "shopping" was the predominant method in Society 1.0. It worked fine because there were fewer people and fewer things people needed; a person aspired to buy only inevitable things. Similarly, the price of possessions was more or less stable and the number of traders was small. Things were easy because what I possessed was always needed by the person next door and vice versa.

The Beginning of Money

As the society progressed to 2.0, the number of parties involved in this transaction grew. For example, John has an extra deer and Rob has extra set of apples. Rob is in a mood to eat some meat, so he goes to John to exchange his apples with the meat. But John already has apples from the day before, so he refuses to accept them. However, he tells Rob that he could use some veggies. Desperate to eat meat, Rob goes to the other side of the town to Carter, the vegetable farmer, hoping he can exchange his apples with fresh eggplants Carter grows and exchange that with the meat John has. Rob gets excited to see the fresh eggplants with Carter, but to his disappointment, Carter doesn't need any apples either. However, he learns that Carter needs a haircut. Now, craving the meat, Rob runs to the barber Bob across the street to see if he could use apples, so Bob can serve Carter, who can give his vegetables in exchange, which Rob could use to get the meat he desperately wants. Fortunately, barber Bob is interested in apples and this tale gets a happy ending, although it took almost a day for Rob to get his bite.

This complexity gave rise to the concept of money, a commonly accepted "commodity value" that made the above process easier. The idea was simple. Everyone exchanged their goods and services with something everyone would want to have. The idea was they could take that commonly accepted "thing" and exchange it for something else they needed because the other person also agreed to exchange her items or services with that common "thing." But defining that common "thing" was diffi-cult because I exchange my goods for something that I don't have to take to someone else for exchanging, otherwise I'll be left with a useless piece of thing without value. Hence, the key is the "value."

Money took several shapes throughout history. At one point, they used cattle as money. Everyone commonly agreed that cattle was useful. I will give you my bag of rice for a cow, which I can take to the farmer and exchange for three bags of vegetables, because the farmer knows he can take the same cow and exchange for something else he wants. The concept of "valuation" also came along as we have seen in this example. One bag of rice was valued at a cow, but the same cow gave three bags of vegetables. So, the cow used to be the olden-day dollar. Or should we say the dollar is the modern-day cow?

But cattle age and they eventually die. If you are one of those unlucky traders who sold all your crops for cattle and then they died before you could exchange them for what you needed, you are sure to go bankrupt in a flash. Society 2.0 experimented with several other forms of money, such as salt, barley, tobacco, shells, buckskin, giant donut-shaped rocks with holes, and even mirrors. All of these "money" had issues and so didn't last long. Imagine the sad stories of folks that possessed the last pieces of money before they changed into something else. What would you do with all that leftover salt? Would it be comparable to what people did in India with old bills when the government trashed its cash and introduced a new set of bills in 2017? Not exactly. Unlike today's paper money, the money back in the day had real value. If you are left with a pile of salt, sell it because salt is a real thing of real value, although it may not be accepted as "money" anymore.

With the discovery of precious metals, everyone agreed that metals had value in their life, which gave rise to coins as money. For example, silver coins were once used as currency. I sell my goods or services for a certain number of coins and I will take them to buy something else I want. If I make more coins than I use, I have some savings built for a rainy day. While silver, bronze, copper, and gold were all used for coin-based currency, gold became the standard toward the last quarter of Society 2.0. Gold became so standardized it entered into the English language as "gold standard"—something superior to take reference from, a well-deserved linguistic tribute. Gold is still considered a metal of substantial value. Even when we do not use gold as currency, everyone accepts it as money because it will always have a buyer and a price in the foreseeable future, though its price fluctuates over time but well within expectations.

The Olden-Day Bankers: Goldsmiths

A rich farmer sells his crop for a bunch of gold coins and saves those coins in his bedroom. This would pose a risk of robbery today and this posed a risk of robbery then. It's one of the things that never changed.

So, what did people do with excess gold coins? They saved them with goldsmiths. Banks are nothing but olden-day goldsmiths who would issue a receipt for the gold coins they received in the form of a "paper note." That butcher who saved those extra gold coins can take his note to the goldsmith whenever he wished and could get his gold coins back. Goldsmiths charged a nominal fee for safely storing everyone's gold coins.

Over time, goldsmiths realized that not many people were going back to get all their gold coins, leaving them with a stock pile of gold. Smart goldsmiths realized there was nothing stopping them to lend some coins to people in need, of course for a fee. That way, they could make money from both hands, and they did exactly that. They had enough coins in their possession that they could safely issue them as loans. They kept a certain portion of it in case any "depositor" came back with their note to claim their coins. This led to the concept of modern-day banks where you save your gold, that is, money, and the bank lends that to people in need for a fee called interest. The receipt notes goldsmiths issued evolved into the modern-day cash. However, there is one big difference between these two. Can you figure what that is? I will hop back to this shortly.

Fractional Reserve Banking

Gradually, the notes goldsmiths issued were accepted by everyone because they knew they can go back to the goldsmith anytime and change them for gold coins. So, they started issuing notes instead of coins for those taking loans as well. However, the fee they were getting from the loans was very attractive. That, together with the fact that only a few people were coming back to collect their gold coins, allowed them to give away more "loans" than the value of the gold coins they had at any given time. This whole phenomenon gave rise to the modern-day economy, especially the fact that there is more "debt" in circulation today than actual money reserve—a phenomenon called fractional reserve banking—and it started to fill with more debt compared to the available gold coins. In this scenario, goldsmiths would get in trouble if everyone with the notes issued by them came back to collect their gold coins, because they simply didn't have enough coins to back all the notes they issued.

By the same token, today's problem is not the lack of debt, but that our economy will be in trouble if everyone decides to pay back all the debt, because there is simply not enough cash to meet all the debt.

All this happened in the later part of Society 2.0 where the economies were built by and revolved around gold. History taught us that a lot of wars have been fought for this precious metal. Kingdoms were valued by the amount of gold they possessed.

Transition to Modern-Day Banking

The trajectory from the goldsmith bankers to the modern-day financial system is complicated, with most of it taking place in the industrial society, Society 3.0. The simplest way to look at it is these goldsmiths emerged into banks and notes turned into currency. With so many goldsmiths in existence, a note issued by one goldsmith may or may not be accepted by others. Goldsmiths started to form a group, accepting each other's notes, starting a banking system. But what about a goldsmith in another city altogether? Well, people were not moving long distances so this wasn't a major problem until trade started to expand, forcing people to mobilize more. You are short of cash in a new town? Sorry, you should have planned better.

There was another major problem with this system. It worked as long as people trusted the goldsmith. The moment word goes out that there were more "notes" in circulation than the actual gold coins, everyone rushed to the goldsmith to get their coins back. These problems, together with some governments' monstrous debt after wars, created the need to control money centrally thus giving rise to the concept of central gold-smiths a.k.a. central banks. Hence, the central bank became the bank for other banks. Banking started by goldsmiths simply providing safety to people's coins emerged into a full-on financial system.

The Gold Standard

With every country having their own currency, controlled by respective governments, how do you calculate the exchange rate? If I travel to Argentina carrying U.S. dollars, how many Argentinian pesos do I get? One? 10? 100? What determines that number? As you can see, there was a need for a common standard. Using the same logic as our olden-day banks: goldsmiths, every country mapped their currency to gold, determining the value of their currency. Their paper currency is mapped to their gold reserves, which in turn drive the value of the currency. For example, if you have one kilogram of gold and you print 1,000 pesos, each peso is worth one gram. If the United States has one kilogram of gold and they print 100 dollars, each dollar is worth 10 grams. Using this logic, 1 U.S. dollar gets me 10 pesos. If you need more money, no problem. Print it. But the amount of gold you carry is not changing, causing the paper currency to value less. This phenomenon is called the "gold standard."

This worked fine for a while, but world wars changed everything. Several countries spent endless amount of money on wars forcing them to print more money to fund them. They soon realized that the gold standard limited their ability to print money, and for the same reason countries started to move away from it. United States, on the other hand, did relatively well, especially during World War I. Its global trade brought most of the world's gold reserves to the country, leaving the United States with plenty of gold supplies. That allowed the United States to continue to back their dollars with their gold reserves, which were pretty strong. As gold reserves shifted to the United States, most other global economies couldn't sustain any longer mapping their currencies to their depleting gold reserves. They were looking for a solution. In 1944, a conference held among countries reached an agreement to map their currency to U.S. dollar instead of gold and was called the Bretton Woods Agreement (CFI Team 2022). The U.S. dollar was in turn mapped to gold due to its strong gold reserves, making it the new global standard. However, U.S. dollar–gold mapping, too, didn't last longer. Several wars, primarily the World War II (Ghizoni 2013), weakened the U.S. dollar as well. Finally, in 1971, the then U.S. President Richard Nixon decided to take the U.S. dollar off the gold ending the 27 years of association (ibid CFI Team). What does that mean? Most global currencies are pegged to the U.S. dollar and the U.S. dollar in turn is pegged to nothing.

Think about what this entails. The millions of dollars you have under your mattress is not "guaranteed" to get you anything, unless that paper is recognized to possess any value, because it is no longer mapped to anything of value. We all agree that the paper in our pockets has value because it's backed by an entity we all rely on: the government.

So, today's financial system runs on trust. One event that shakes peoples' trust shakes the entire financial market as people are worried the "value" of money will go down because everyone would start panicking. One tweet by a prominent person has the potential to tumble the stock market and even tank the economy. This wouldn't have happened back in the day because the value of money was always guaranteed by something material. This transformation in money is relatively new. It occurred only in 1971, a few decades ago, almost before we began to enter the information society.

Let me remind you that financial services industry is extremely broad and complex with subsectors—each being a beast by itself. Banks that started small grew into large-scale financial institutions in the industrial society, many offering a wide range of financial services such as retail banking, investment services and wealth management, insurance, corporate banking, investment banking, and tax and audit. Financial services is a massive industry with each subsector a beast on its own. For simplicity, we shall focus on the side of the industry you and I deal with daily. However, they all had one thing in common: the human touch.

If you want to deposit cash, you head to a bank and hand over your cash to the teller; the teller counts the money by hand and gives you a passbook that tells you how much deposit you have. You securely keep that passbook, go back to the same bank, hand over the passbook, fill a form with withdrawal details, and submit that form to the teller. You get the money and the passbook gets updated. You want to buy insurance?

Contact an insurance agent. Want to invest? Visit a broker. Need a loan? Go to a loan agent.

An important invention in the 1950s revolutionized the lives of tellers and financial industry's speed and accuracy of doing work: cash counting machines. Then came another major revolution that threatened the livelihoods of a lot of cashiers across the globe: the automated teller machines (ATMs), the same "money robots" or "robot-banks" we use today to deposit as well as withdraw cash. ATMs surely disrupted retail banking. In fact, ATMs are the retail banks when it comes to checking and savings. How often do we go inside a bank these days for these primitive transactions?

This was just the beginning of the financial services industry disruption. The major disruption came along in the form of what's known as the fintech revolution, which uses technology to the fullest to bring innovation to customers. Arguably, this took the money to the next level, taking money further away from anything of substance to simply 0s and 1s. People these days transfer these digits to each other rather than actual money. And this trend has gone fully digital with events such as the COVID-19 pandemic. When I'm with my corporate partners, I often joke around saying money has been E=mc-ed, that is, converted from matter to invisible entity. Once used to be in the form of goods and services, money took several other forms such as salt, shells, and silver to finally settle for gold, then evolved into paper only to become invisible.

The beginnings of fintech were marked by traditional banks when they began providing online access to accounts, bringing technology to interact with users, in addition to supporting back-end functions. The big step forward was arguably marked by PayPal through its ability to transfer money online across multiple banking institutions, breaking the biggest barrier of financial services industry. Call it an abstract layer on top of all banks.

The concept was such a major hit. It not only gave rise to so many firms specialized in online money transfer, but also evolved to merge money and social activities. If you ask around, many people across the globe may not know Citibank or any other financial institutions, but most people know tech giants such as Google and Apple. Google Pay and Apple Pay replaced cash-based retail transactions and brought more people into this global financial ecosystem. E-commerce giants like Alibaba also entered the fintech world through their specialized services such as Alipay.

Taking online bank account access to the next level, online-only banks such as Marcus emerged. Traditional banks improved their online banking capabilities. To compete with the abstract layer built for money transfer, such as PayPal, on top of them, they partnered with services like Zelle. There may not be physical banks in remote parts of the world due to infrastructure limitations, but most people today have access to the Internet. Online banks made banking accessible to more people.

But fintech revolution didn't stop at online banking and transfers. Companies like Acorn transformed the wealth management sector. There are numerous investment options in emerging fintech startups, catering to all kinds of investors out there, all of them fighting to get customers, encouraging more people to get into the investment business. On the side, online mortgage lenders such as AimLoan transformed the mortgage industry. Insurance industry has mostly gone online these days. When was the last time you visited a physical store to file your taxes? When was the last time you went door to door to raise funds for that charitable cause?

So, is fintech all about brining financial services online? Definitely not. That's just the beginning of fintech revolution. It's all about utilizing technology to bringing value through innovation. For instance, wealth management companies use AI-based robo-investors to study market trends and invest smartly. These companies invite investors to grab such markets and often send notifications. Well before the pandemic hit, I too had received a notification to invest in Zoom. Smart invest-bots round up your spending, take that small change from each spend, and invest it for you to grow your change into something substantial.

Robo-brokers analyze your financial situation much better than any human can and provide you with a wealth management roadmap no humans can provide. Auto insurance robots track driving patterns, understand personalities, assess risk, and can devise a customized quote better than any human can. If you are driving safe and driving less, you get a check for being a good driver. Mortgage-bots can process thousands of documents, analyze your financial situation, and assess the level of risk much more accurately, much better than your credit score can reveal. The list can go on. If these are all happening today, where do you think financial services industry is heading from here? Here are a few trends.

Advanced Risk Tackling Machines (RTM)

If you haven't figured out by now, financial services industry runs on tackling risks. In a way, it's a euphemistic pseudonym for risk management industry.

All businesses look out for risk sources. First, for lenders, the biggest risk is repayment of the debt by the borrower. A careful and detailed analysis must be done before lending. It's not just the borrower's financial situation that counts; his or her behavioral patterns and market trends among other things are also equally important consideration parameters. Wealth management is all about predicting market trends. Among many types which excel at predicting, insurance companies are the smartest— the biggest of risk management firms.

The value of money itself depends on everyone's agreement that it has value, as we have seen earlier. This keeps public confidence intact. Advanced risk management is key to the well-being of this industry. Advanced bots help detect risks and mitigate them before they turn into issues, for both the financial institutions and the consumers. The Zoom stock prediction I pointed out earlier will be primitive compared to future advanced risk management.

Banks as Experience Centers

With all the online banking revolutions, everyone has a big question. What is the future of banks and what is the future of bank employees? Teller transactions will grow smaller in number. Banks will turn into places to socialize, experience financial products, and receive financial services such as investment advice among others. The power of physical contact cannot be underestimated and hence there will always be a place for face-to-face contact, although it's neither going to be the same as the past nor will occur at the same scale. This means retail banks will turn into experience and entertainment centers while most of the day-to-day transactions take place in the digital world.

Smart Advisors

If anyone (or anything) can offer you the best financial advice by analyzing your financial health, it'll be personal digital robo-assistants. Money, being such an integral part of our life, will be integrated into other parts of day-to-day automation as well. These smart money advisors will be integrated into all walks of life even through smart assistants such as Amazon Alexa.

Digital Currency

A new flower arrived in the Netherlands in the 17th century, the tulip. It was so beautiful and special; everyone fell in love with it. The newcomer encouraged a public interest in this brand-new flower. Everyone wanted to have one of these. Tulips turned into a great business. Then, a lucky tulip farmer was able to produce dotted tulips by accident. They sold for more. That accident was later found to be caused by an infection. But it didn't matter because rare things tend to up their value. The fear of missing out (FOMO) forced everyone to jump on this tulip bandwagon: tulips at one point were sold for the price of a mansion (Hayes 2022). People exchanged their houses for a tulip, which they later realized was nothing but a house of cards that simply crashed. I would like to rest my case on crypto here but let me elaborate a bit for those millions of crypto enthusiasts.

The context: crypto enthusiasts argue and believe that it will be the new form of currency. Let's remind ourselves that currency used to be representative of something physical until the U.S. dollar had been taken off the gold standard, making currencies fiat, backed by respective governments and their economies. However, crypto is a fiat currency as well and it has value because people believe it has value, thus defeating one of the fundamental reasons for moving off currencies like the U.S. dollar.

A reckless government could tank the value of their currency as it happened in a few countries already and some argue that it makes a case for crypto. Citizens of countries with such challenges do look for an alternative currency, but is that force sufficient to make a global change? Countries with stable currencies drive the global "economy" after all. Is it possible for a large number of countries to tank their economies? Chances are thin as the global economy is relative. Even if crypto is to become the new standard, it won't be without heavy regulations that will defeat the whole "democratization" of currency. Besides, management of global economy by a set of people sounds like a good concept, but it will be impractical as fluctuations may be frequent, significantly impacting the lives of billions.

Another argument for crypto is that it is digital and there is a good place for digital currency. However, I would argue that money has already gone digital. As we discussed earlier, how often do we handle paper cash? Rarely. Will we manage digital currency using blockchain technology, the same technology used for bitcoin? Probably. Venezuela released their new digital currency called Petro Coin on the blockchain platform, for example. Interestingly, this coin is backed by their oil reserves to grow confidence in the country's currency that has lost nearly all its value. The key here is this currency is government managed and backed by the country's reserves. The only thing it has in common with bitcoin is the platform it runs on.

There will be other localized "digital coins" that can be earned through certain activities and redeemed for certain products or services. Health coins to reward participation in certain health care-related activities that can be redeemed for health care-related services as seen in Falcon's story are an example. However, these coins can be seen as an extension to various rewards programs we are already used to.

Please note that crypto currency may have a role to play in the future, especially given its underlying platform and the adaptation rate. For example, the health coin program we just referenced could be run as a smart contract on blockchain that pays in crypto. These coins could be redeemed for other services or "cash out" where it's allowed.

All that said, will currency completely become digital in the future? Will the United States release a dollar coin? It's possible. Watching this space can make as big a difference as a decision made early, although it won't be like cryptocurrency. Money, as we know, has been changing and will continue to change. It may endure to the point it becomes completely invisible.

Merger With Other Industries

This is a big one. Financial services industry will no longer be this secluded especially with big players with the likes of Goldman Sachs. We have already seen how young fintech companies took a share of this market. The market has been so ripe that big tech companies such as Google, Apple, and Alibaba have jumped into the game through their respective Google Pay, Apple Pay, and Alipay services. These companies have an already built empire of their dedicated, loyal customers. Why not use that access to provide services around something everyone needs every day— money. Adoption by these big players ensured that people with Internet but without bank access were also going to fruit from this cashless economy. It is going to evolve further with various other industries expanding their businesses to overlap with this sector. The reverse merger will also occur through banks turning into entertainment and retail centers.

What if your car will turn into a bank in the future, for example? Or your coffee maker, washing machine, or even the refrigerator? Let me cite an example. If you're a part of the Starbucks reward program, you can load your Starbucks account with some money, meaning you are saving with Starbucks "bank." You cannot withdraw cash in most circumstances but you can use that in exchange for their products—helpful if you're an avid coffee lover. That's interest-free loan for Starbucks which it can redirect for further business growth. Apply similar logic to a car that can start a bank where you can load money to pay your bills as you drive around town. It's not just for expenses. The future self-driving car that will turn into a taxi when not in use will load its bank with that money as well. Your smart refrigerator bank will use that money to fund the groceries it will self-order. You want to round off each spend to the nearest dollar and invest in the stock market? Your refrigerator can do it for you. Watch out for this interesting trend. I strongly believe this is in the future of our money and will happen in our lifetime.

Again, what's in it for you? There will soon be a day when your industry will cross paths with financial services sector if it hasn't already. Being prepared is the only and the most secure harness you can carry in this climb of uncertainty. Understand this sector; read as many books; listen to market pundits—if you're planning to join the fintech revolution as it is here to grow. I personally think technology has barely scratched the surface of financial services industry. If you're planning to join the finance revolution, you must understand technology, at least how it works. Understanding technology in finances is so inevitable, it won't do to shrug this inevitability with "that's not my expertise." Whether you work in the financial services industry or own a business in this field, add tech to your industry today. If not, I can guarantee that in near future you will be doing something else other than this.

Future of Shopping (and Trade)

Shopping is the most favorite pass time for a lot of people. It's so essential indicator of the country's economy that it defines its GDP. The more you spend, the more money gets circulated in the economy and healthier the GDP would be. It's not a surprise that shopping has been around since the early human days, that is, Society 1.0, though the shape and form was entirely different. If you want to buy something today, you visit a store physically or virtually and pay through a medium, either paper or digital. Money and goods' stores, however, were not a thing back in the day.

If you went back to those times to buy things, people would expect you to bring something they desperately need in exchange with theirs. We covered this barter system in detail under the section "money." Imagine bartering in a shopping mall today. Think about what you do for living and draw a line from that to what you want to buy on a day-to-day basis. Tell me how long you think it would take to find the products you need. You can imagine how complicated shopping would be. It was only after money was invented that buying and selling became simplistic. With rise in global trade, the concept of stores evolved in the later part of the agricultural society with mom and pop shops that later evolved into stores where owners didn't have to produce anything on their own, but rather could become intermediaries. They no longer had to be a butcher to sell meat, farmer to sell vegetables, or an artist to sell an art collection.

Industrial revolution then ultimately transformed shopping. Mass production of goods changed the way stores worked. Goods were produced in factories and distributed to multiple stores that sold those products to their customers for a profit. But stores were still those places in the early part of industrial society where different products were stocked. People visited them with a list to fetch goods; the shopkeeper packed the goods and gave it to you. They're still prevalent in various parts of the world even today.

Then came along buffet shopping where you could pick the products you wanted and pay at the end of your shopping. These self-service stores further evolved into departmental stores that sold a large number of products and mega supermarkets, with even larger stock of products. The buffet shopping ushered into a new era of industry called packaging because the products had to be enticing enough to grab people's attention. The look and feel of the product, the branding, became as important as the product itself. And this transformation happened only well within the past century.

Many people admit that the next revolution that transformed buying as an experience happened in the shopping malls, which converted the mind-numbing task of buying into endorphin- and dopamine-releasing experience. The giant structures in these malls offered entertainment alongside shopping. The investors looked into what people did alongside when they go outside their homes for shopping. Unlike the old days when people had to spend a lot of time visiting dozens of places for buying dozens of stuffs, people could buy those items within a couple of hundred to thousands of square yards, saving a lot of time for other forms of entertainment—food, games, movies, shows, fitness centers, and the like. These malls converted shopping into family activity centers. Departmental stores and supermarkets made their way into these shopping malls. They catered to both people who go to shopping and opt for entertainment on the side and those who go for entertainment and shop on the side. There was one common thing: shopping.

Soon, to the delight of many and dismay of some, information technology quickly found its way into shopping, eliminating the need to visit the physical stores time and again. This single event disrupted every brick-and-mortar store across the world. You no longer need to drive up to a store to buy that favorite jacket. You can simply order it online from the comfort of your bed and boom, it's at your doorstep. Physical stores don't survive independently any longer without online presence. Every brick-and-mortar store now has an online counterpart. The ones that didn't transform themselves enough went bankrupt. How many blockbuster stores do you see in 2021? Zero. That's the key revolution Society 4.0 brought along and that's where all developed societies are today.

The days are gone when you were compelled to search for a particular physical store to buy a product you saw the advertisement of in the television. Social media revolution further changed the way we shop. You will be able to buy a product as soon as you see it on Facebook, before it fades away from your memory or interest. Neither companies will force you to visit their website nor their store to purchase it. Products are just a click away.

The question is where do we go from here? Will online business replace brick-and-mortar stores, or will they merely shatter their dominance? What is the future of shopping malls? How will automation change shopping? How soon will goods be delivered once ordered online? There are several questions to be answered. Here are the top shopping trends that might interest you.

Omni-Channel

As we saw before, shopping moved from in-stores to online in the information society. More online channels have emerged outside of retail online stores. This model will evolve to make shopping an omni-channel experience. You may come across a product on your Instagram feed. You may want to see and feel it before you buy, so you go to a near-by store and check it out. You come back home, do some web research on it to understand its features, and check the reviews. You then want to get some more first-hand thoughts about it so you create a post on Facebook asking for recommendations. You're content with what your community suggested so you ask your virtual assistant to order it. From researching for this product that began a week ago to jumping onto multiple platforms before it converted into a sale, companies must maintain their value-presence almost everywhere, even in customer's satisfaction and feedback platforms. While this may not mean much to the customer, there is a lot of burden on the manufacturer and/or the retailer to convert that interest you showed a week ago on the Instagram post to a sale closure on Amazon Alexa a week later. This is essential because these end-to-end insights help organizations make several decisions. The sale rate cannot be determined by sales through Instagram. The ad-spend on social media resulted in a sale elsewhere a week later. You might have clicked on that link, went to a store, checked the product out, and forgotten about it. But for the manufacturer, you are a potential customer, and they can gently remind you of their product, perhaps through sending an e-mail. Even better, they may decide to give you a 10 percent off to motivate you to buy. What this means is your activity across all these channels must be tracked to accurately get insights about you. That's exactly how it is going to work in the future and some of this end-to-end tracking has already begun, thanks to IoB (Internet of Behaviors).

This phenomenon has a name. It's called e-commerce, not electronic, the one you're familiar with but everywhere. It's everywhere-commerce. Granted that it has its own downsides to it: this is a direct threat to user's privacy, but that is a discussion on a whole new level that crosses domains across business ethics, principle of pleasure (whatever that is), and user statistics.

Smart Shopping

What if your virtual assistant replies "I recommend you wait until next month to buy Oculus Quest 2. You had some unforeseen expenses this month." Or even better, "Are you sure you want to buy? Based on past trends, there is a good chance Oculus Quest 2 will go on sale next month." What's happening here is you're letting your virtual assistant do all the analysis-heavy lifting, so you don't have to. This functionality requires the integration of multiple channels that can be ultimately fed to the assistant.

Zero Thinking

How often do you go beyond the list of videos recommended by YouTube? At least, it rarely happens with me. The list of videos presented to a viewer based on her interests, past viewing habits, subscriptions, and so on feels like we've been searching for them; at least most of them do. A list keeps playing and I rarely change what gets played to me.

We're suddenly talking about entertainment because it is also a type of shopping. You are "shopping" for entertainment and it's getting presented to you without much "thinking" from your part. But, apply the same model of "zero-thinking" to any shopping and that's the future. Once shopping used to be a chore people like me hated. Thanks to online commerce, shopping turned into a zero-effort activity. Now, take that one step further. The future of shopping is zero-thinking, meaning you don't need to put substantial efforts to think about what to buy. AI does it for you. Look at it like an extension of "products you may also like" from your online retailer. Your shopping trends are tracked to predetermine your future shopping needs. All you need to do is confirm. For example, did Amazon ever remind you to reorder that hair-gel because it's already been 45 days or so, based on your past trends? You will see more and more of it in the future.

This is all about taking the stress of decision making away from the customers and applying to any industry serving them. A bakery getting your bread ready every day without having to explicitly order, changing flavors based on your preferences to surprise you, throwing in that coffee you like, or even surprising you with new flavors if you're willing are all examples of zero-thinking shopping. Since the process makes a customer's life easier—especially the ones who're always on the fence while deciding—they appreciate it. In some cases, they become the customers for life. But it doesn't mean the process should be entirely without human intervention. A confirmation message could be sent to ensure you need the bread today to avoid waste, in case you are out of town.

Moving to a subscription-based model instead of the "pay-per-use" paradigm to blow your mind with a surprise product every day sounds like the next-generation customer relation building method. Even if you are not "surprised," you don't have to think about where to go for your needs. One less thing for you to worry about. Take Panera bread, for example. They have a monthly subscription that gives you unlimited coffee. Such models ensure that you no longer be unable to decide where to grab your coffee but ask for it without hassles. Combining customer loyalty and personalized service to move to a zero-thinking model is the future of customer experience, including shopping.

Experience Centers

So many stores have closed down owing to disruption by online stores in the last few years. On the other hand, e-commerce businesses have soared like rockets. Amazon grew from a $36 billion company in 2009 to $1.2 trillion in August 2022 ("Amazon Net Worth" 2022). COVID-19 pandemic has added more insult to this injury. With this online trend, there are several questions around the existence of physical stores. Will they completely disappear one day? The answer is absolutely not. For instance, Amazon has begun to move to brick-and-mortar from full online model through Amazon Go, Amazon 4-Star, Amazon Fresh, Amazon Books, and Amazon Pop Up. No wonder this online–offline model will rejigger themselves with customer demand. But online presence will undoubtedly continue to grow, and as mentioned earlier, physical stores will turn more and more into experience centers. They will turn into go-feel stores with products and experience, not necessarily the only places you buy things from. You will see more entertainment options in most stores. Baristas and bars inside of grocery stores are just an example. For independent store owners, say in electronics, it is essential to join the larger ecosystem to track user activities and get the fair share of the profit made at the end. That's because their store may have played a key role in that TV you bought online as you checked it out in their store. This is currently an issue and haven't been figured out yet. If we flip it, there's an opportunity for entrepreneurs.

Goodbye Cashiers

Business models like Amazon Go stores are already gaining a lot of traction, enough to follow suit by many others as a futurist model for a retail store. You walk in, pick what you want, and walk out. All products carry sensors to identify themselves, and robots (physical or virtual) will help you with questions You either shop using a smart shopping cart that calculates the total and charges your credit card on file or a smart self-checkout desk to read all the products, calculate the total, and enable you to pay with your palm. These stores will still have baristas and other entertainment options. You can hang out however long you wish. You pay when you finally decide to leave the store. This, however, doesn't mean stores will be entirely cashier-free. There will be limited number of staff to supervise and to provide customer support. Meaning, cashiers will be present to handle exceptions, while machines will present themselves as day-to-day cashiers and helpers.

Next-Generation At-Home Shopping

AR, without a doubt, can be declared as the dominant technology that will enable us to try products from the comfort of our couch. Are you considering buying a new sofa? AR will simulate that sofa and take you to your virtual living room with it. It will feel so real, you will find this option better than shopping in the store. After all, you need to rely on your imagination on how that sofa will look if you visit a store. By the way, if you've never tried any of the immersion technologies, it's high time you do. And who knows, that might be the right moment you decide to incorporate the idea into your business.

E-Mailed Products, No Shipping Required

A beautiful 3D art on the Internet or a store can reach your home without even carrying it. Instead of asking for your physical address, you simply provide your e-mail. The art company e-mails you the product which you print on your 3D printer at home. E-mailing physical products is just a step away from the technology that's close to maturity. Clothes, jewelry, artwork, toys, and musical instruments—you name it. You will be able to e-mail a lot of products in the future.

Delivery in Minutes

Of course, products will be delivered in minutes if they are e-mailed. But not all products can be printed at home. We only wish we can print fresh vegetables, right? Products ordered online will be at your doorstep within minutes in the future. How? First, the warehouses they get stored will come closer to your home, reducing the distance they need to travel. Instead of large warehouses across thousands of acres in the outskirts, imagine multilayered warehouses closer to the population. There will also be floating warehouses in the sky. So, the product you order will now come out of a warehouse within a few miles as compared to thousands of miles. Second, packages will be air-dropped through a drone instead of a driver spending all that time on the road. These delivery drones—and if you're worried they can't fly for long—need not be nuclear powered because warehouses are closer to homes. Even if the drone needs to make a longer trip, it will stop by a charging station installed on the top of an electricity pole. If all drones are busy assisting other customers, a land robot will pick up the task, walk over on the sidewalk, and deliver the package to you. This is not just a concept. Amazon is already moving on a lot of these, claiming to deliver packages up to five pounds in 30 minutes or less using small drones.

More Personalized Service

When we go shopping, how many products do you explore before settling on that one pair of jeans you like or the beautiful sandal? Probably a lot. We buy what we buy for several reasons and we do not buy the rest for different other reasons. Today, stores keep track of what we buy through what has been scanned at the cashier but what about all the products we didn't buy? What if we are persuaded to buy them in the future? I am sure you would appreciate an e-mail that the lovely jacket you tried on is 50 percent off which you'd respectfully kept back on seeing the price tag. We will see this next level of shopping in the future. How do they track our activity as we try things on? Various techniques can be deployed, such as a combination of sensors and computer vision. AI algorithms will be able to make an educated guess on the reasons behind not buying certain products—an easy one if you keep the product back immediately after viewing the price tag and fix your eyes on it for an instant or maybe look back. We'd not mind getting personalized shopping notifications based on our behavior in the store. Instead, the challenge here is the enormous amount of data that generate and the back-and-forth which strains the network. However, edge computing, that brings computing closer to where the data are produced, can be a solution.

Cloud Kitchens

No discussion about shopping will be complete without talking about shopping for one of the most basic necessities—food: specifically cooked food, serviced by food services industry. Of course, we buy cooked food from restaurants, which range from a neighbor selling homemade food to fancy restaurants serving decorative delicacies. This foodservice industry is projected to produce an annual revenue of around $898 billion alone in the United States, according to restaurant.org (2022). Even food retailers, such as grocery stores, have decided to get a bite of this pie through selling cooked food. However, this is one of the industries that was disrupted heavily by the COVID-19 pandemic. We witnessed several restaurants being shut down and food delivery services picking up a lot of steam. Will indoor dining come back to full speed? Will food delivery services continue or slow down post pandemic?

First, I strongly believe that there's no way food services industry, specifically indoor dining, will die out. Nothing can beat the experience of eating in a restaurant and getting "serviced." However, the key here is the word "service." Restaurants that focus on providing good service to customers will do just fine. Meanwhile, food delivery business is here to stay as well. Those looking for delicious meals but either do not care about service or are lazy to dine out will resort to delivery services. With the growth in this industry, how will restaurants maximize their share of this pie by expanding their presence? Will they open franchises everywhere?

The solution lies in a trending concept called the cloud kitchen. The idea is multiple restaurants share a kitchen to cater to the local delivery demand. If I am a famous pizza maker from New York and I want to expand my business to California, I would rent a part of a kitchen in San Francisco to bake my pizza which I may be sharing with several other restaurants. These restaurants will not only share the amenities, but they could be sharing a chef too. The chef must be trained to cook recipes from multiple restaurants. This is a win for restaurant owners as they can expand their presence and a win for customers as well as they will now have access to delicacies they previously didn't have. This trend is beginning and it has a huge potential in the future. If you're an investor, this might be the right horse to ride.

The shopping industry is changing rapidly. It's not just the retail industry, the front end for shopping, the dynamics of wholesale and trade in general are changing. There is more emphasis on manufacturing locally. That not only helps the economy but allows less transportation time, thus resulting in greener supply chains. Retail may be transforming completely as we have seen but what does it mean to you? The 21st-century shopper needs to understand the shopping trends and become an intelligent buyer, making use of all the tools available. And if you are in the shopping industry, you better get on this "connected shopping" bandwagon, else you'll risk losing your business. For entrepreneurs, however, opportunities are endless in this space.

Future of Travel: Transportation and Hospitality

People love to travel, whether for work or to stroll. Their need to travel defines their need to change. While it may seem trivial to talk much about travel because it has truly become an everyday activity, none other than people living before 2020 can tell how important it is for them to be able to move, owing to the pandemic. People were stuck at home, not even traveling distances their legs could afford.

The history of travel is as interesting as places to travel. In the past, people ate whatever food they found in walking distance, whether tree-grown or hunted. As society learnt systematic food growing, the concept of markets matured and buying capacity heightened. Customers nearby could no longer buy all the items produced, so the need to travel farther grew. If there's one thing that better defines the history of human civilization, it's their tendency to move from one place to another. We figured out ways to use animals as transport vehicles for people as well as goods. Then, one of the greatest inventions in the history of humanity shattered the limits of our meager physical bodies and deemed us global in true sense. It was the invention of the wheel and transport vehicles. Wheels complimented the animals so they lugged goods with less effort and formed more complex vehicles such as carts.

Our quest to improve forced us to push our boundaries further. Transportation within each society became more efficient; we became more curious about other societies and so visited them, often with wrath and rampage and especially with a goal to steal the resources they possessed, if not to wipe them altogether, each time. When carts traversed the lands, we wondered how it was to drive them in water. Then came boats and ships and reached societies separated by water, giving rise to global trade. All of these were powered by beautiful natural energies such as wind and organic food eaten by animals. These were the best transportation options in Society 2.0.

One of the reasons why people needed robust vehicles was wheels rotated so faster their carriages could not keep up with the speed. Thanks to the metallurgical innovation of the industrial revolution, manufacturing of various metallic parts was then possible. That helped build the early-day automobiles and trains. The first engines ran with steam and the subsequent ones burnt fuels inside and were called combustion engines. As powerful as multiple horses, these combustion engines made private to semiprivate long-distance travel easier. And with the advent of bigger cars (buses) for long-distance journeys, trains for even longer, and motor-powered ships for faster travel on water, people could finally stride across the globe. Then came along two brothers who gave wings to the car. Gravity watched in awe as people flew higher and farther crossing fields, villages, cities, and oceans. The Wright-brothers-given set of tools inspired air-cars (helicopters) and air-buses (airplanes) that further shrunk this world, allowing us to travel across the globe in hours, as compared to months and even years, at some point.

This fast development in transportation options opened up gates wider for worldwide exchange of goods. Goods transported across the globe faster, and most importantly cheaper. Manufacturing didn't have to be done locally anymore. People could produce goods in one part of the world and transport them effectively to another, complimenting each other's incapacity. Countries traded more, thus diversifying options. It was possible for a global citizen that her favorite mango from the farms of Peru, plucked yesterday, could land in the United States today. With the expanding transportation industry in Society 3.0, it also opened up doors for people to travel for fun. These together with the economic growth caused by the industrial revolution and changes in employment policies such as mandatory vacation time among others gave rise to the hospitality industry, such as hotels and resorts.

The availability of cheap and fast shipping options meant that not only the goods produced in a country could be transported to other countries, outsource manufacturing of goods could also occur, meaning that businesses could build a plant and hire a team from a different country. The phones we use in the United States do not have to be manufactured here if it costs more. Manufacturing could be outsourced to places with low cost of production, bigger workforce, and cheaper raw materials, along with government incentives, for example, China. Likewise, the cotton that make clothes in the United States can be grown in India, shipped to Bangladesh, stitched in there to make clothes, and then shipped back to the United States. This outsourcing changed the economic balance of the world. Outsourcing has its own up and downsides. Let's not get into that debate now, but it's an objective observation to say that the world has transformed.

Growth in the aerospace technology created safer and bigger aircrafts, improving global travel. Hotels chained themselves worldwide, catering to both domestic and international travelers. Some areas evolved as tourist centers, with their economies highly dependent on tourism revenue. This also strengthened outsourcing as people could travel throughout the world in the matter of hours to understand the requirements of the product. There are no longer rigid language barriers which prevent partnerships. After bridging the gap in their understanding of what needs to be built, entrepreneurs can go back to their home country to work instantly on it.

A trend that was moving in this direction got a major boost in the information society, Society 4.0. Enterprise resource planning (ERP) systems like SAP brought in efficiencies to complex global goods and people transport processes. Growth in the digital world, with 24×7 dedicated Internet, made customer reach, transportation, and accommodation booking easy. It skyrocketed the global travel and hospitality industries. You book a vacation package online with a few clicks and complete a trip to Bali. You can schedule a package shipment online; your package will be collected from your home and sent to its destination, giving you real-time status along the way.

The further revolutions disrupted the industry so drastically that it led to both gain and loss of thousands of jobs. Travel tech companies like Uber disrupted a sector within the travel industry by democratizing the taxi business. Companies like Turo disrupted another sector of the travel industry by democratizing the rental car industry. Hospitality tech companies like Airbnb disrupted the hospitality industry: anyone with a spare room can play a hotel owner by renting it out for short durations, and anyone with time on their hands can become a tour guide. The transformation the information society brought along, just in the past decade, is phenomenal. That's where we are now. Where does travel, transportation, and hospitality go from here? Here are the key trends:

Autonomous Cars

Autonomous cars are not any future inventions; they are here already. I have been driving a Tesla for a few years now. I should rather say a Tesla has been driving me. Haven't we done enough of this "autonomous" talk in the previous chapter? Let me just say this: it's not just going to be about cars. Buses, vans, and trucks are all in the verge of going autonomous with many companies such as Volvo, Tesla, and Daimler already on the lane. There are many more joining. Takeaway: this trend is here to stay.

Autonomous Hotels and Restaurants

Imagine you walk into a hotel and are greeted by a robot that recognizes you by your face, welcomes you by your name, checks you in automatically, and takes you to your room. You suddenly realize you forgot to bring your toiletry kit. You call through your smartphone hotel app, asking for room service, and a robot comes to your aid. Your robot chef will prepare the food for you and your server robot will bring it to your table. Moley, a company that's headed to sell ceiling-mounted setups called Moley Robotics Kitchen, has fully automatized kitchen work making the preparation of thousands of recipes by a single chef possible. It sounds like science fiction until you land on such place and click an order to see the elegant robotic arm working its way through its recipe or brining your things that you ordered. If you are a frequent traveler, it's likely you stumbled on one of these at some point. The question of what'll happen to human chefs isn't as distressing as of now, as much as the question of anything old is in risk of substitution by something new.

Autonomous Ports and Stations

You will be greeted by robots in airports. They will not only exchange pleasantries with you, but will provide the assistance you need, such as direction to a particular spot. They will keep an eye on the surroundings to keep airports, train stations, and bus stations safe. The data they gather get processed in real time and security will be notified as soon as any suspected activity is detected. Could that "security" be another bot? One of other areas robots can excel is immigration and customs. Robots got that covered, too. Check-in personnel, gatekeeper, duty-free shopkeeper, conductor, captain, maintenance crew—these are the jobs suited to machines better than humans. Why? Because their productivity never drops with monotonous tasks. And humans can focus on higher productivity tasks.

Traveling With the Sound

I lived in San Francisco but worked in Los Angeles for almost a decade. I traveled every week and spent days away from home because although the air time was only around an hour, the total travel time each way would be close to three hours from door to door. Add flight cancellations and delays on top. It really was an arduous feat to pull long-distance commuting with the existing infrastructure.

Thousands of people can resonate with me when it comes to daily, distant commuting. One of the ways we can solve this problem is using near-vacuum low-pressure "tubes" and pushing a vehicle through it. As rightly as you have guessed, the concept called Hyperloop, an open-source concept developed by Elon Musk, now being undertaken by the Virgin group under the name Virgin Hyperloop, might be a solution to a lot of problems including distant commuting. A few companies are developing and improvising the technology which some call "airplane in a tube." Hyperloop pods can reach the speed of the sound, are deemed safer than airplanes, and look promising though they have their own criticisms. The cost of construction, implications of seismic activities, high-speed traveling experience, pod failures, and security are some of the issues critics are concerned of. However, I believe this technology has an impressive future and sufficient investment is being made into this. Watch this space.

Underground Flying

Do you remember how Falcon reached his doctor's office in San Francisco from his home hundreds of miles away in minutes? He didn't take an airplane, but rather flew underground in his own car in an underground 3D tunnel. Again, we covered this topic earlier and discussed how the Boring Company is making progress with this impressive futuristic roadway. Vehicles converted into temporary autonomous vehicles using car-carrying bins transporting people and goods under the ground are the future for beating traffic jams.

Smart Tourism

There was a time when we paid separately for booking our flight, hotel stay, and transportation. Travel companies now offer vacation packages, incorporating all of them. You may or may not get a good deal but that option is available today. And it exists for a reason. What if we take this connected travel to the next level? Imagine you buy your air, hotel, and rental car from whoever you like, together or separate. These reservations get stored in your calendar. Your personal digital assistant reminds you of your upcoming trip the day before and gives you weather details and travel tips based on the destination data. Probably there is a storm on the horizon you didn't keep track of, a health crisis, or an ongoing coup. The assistant will alert you.

We are just getting started here. You own one of those (upcoming) helper robots? The bot will be smart enough to pack your suitcase depending on your meeting and travel schedule. It (or, he or she) will make sure you have the rain jacket or an umbrella in case the predictions are for a wet day. Taking your spouse along? If you're in a fix where to take your spouse for a romantic dinner, your assistant will suggest a local restaurant that sells the fish you and your partner like—probably the one with 500 5-star ratings. It might book a ride for you ready to pick you on time. Are you one of those who prefer to reach airport only 30 minutes before departure instead of waiting hours? Your assistant will never miss a delayed flight, and if something like that happens, the ride she booked will be notified as well. Your hotel will get the notice, too, so they can redirect the cleaning crew to the ground floor for someone who is arriving earlier than planned. Hotel room is equipped with soft pillows the way you like, thermostat set to 79 degrees, and alarm preset for 7.30 a.m. to give you enough time to get ready for your 10 a.m. meeting.

One of the concerns of this form of arrangement is privacy. Your data will be shared only if you let them with all the parties involved here and will be used only to give you an integrated experience. But in the age of sophisticated data breaches and identity thefts, the systems need to be built with extra layer of data securities in mind.

Space Tourism

"Do you have any plans for next summer?" We often get that question. Instead of "I am going to Peru to see Machu Pichu" or "Rome to see the Coliseum," what if you could say "I am going to see the Earth from the top"? That dream has finally come true. While it's certain that passengers, or rather tourists, have to pay millions of dollars to take their initial journeys to space, with time the cost is expected to come down. You will indisputably be able to say you'd be leaving earth one fine summer (and nobody will assume you're dying) and be back for dinner on earth an hour later.

Space Travel

Space travel is traveling in space to a certain destination as opposed to just visiting the space, taking selfies with the beautiful planet Earth, and being back. With all the advancements in space travel and more and more companies and organizations carrying the baton, namely the government agencies such as NASA and private giants such as SpaceX, Blue Origin and so on, the next few decades' race will undoubtedly be a space race. Exploring the Moon and the Mars are just a few goals. NASA is planning a mission to send humans back to the Moon by 2024, but this time to stay. There are multiple other missions waiting to begin but thought of since decades: the Mars mission, the Near-Earth Asteroids mission, the Europa mission, and so on. We will only see more activity in the years to come. To set the right expectations though, while this activity will grow, it will not be anything more than mere news to watch when there is any major update for common men and women.

Space Transportation

Space transportation is different from space travel. Travel is for people and transportation is for goods. What kind of goods do we send to space? The SpaceX has already declared the cargo plans for its ferrying-to-space missions. It costs $1.1 million for 200 kilograms to travel to the polar orbit with an additional $5.5 thousand per kilogram. In addition, the rates for transportation to mid-inclination low earth orbits, geosynchronous transfer orbit, and trans-lunar injection are also available ("SmallsatRideshare Program" 2020). Goods ridesharing to the space is already existent. In case you want your own robotic probe to space, you can book a flight. Whether you want to send your own camera system to capture videos of space or want to send a special package to your astronaut uncle working on the Moon in the future, carrying out these tasks will be an everyday activity. Be sure to ask for a tracking number though.

Drone and Bot Transportation

As we witnessed in the "future of shopping," companies around the world are striving for goods delivery in 30 minutes or less. The transportation of goods will soon take autonomous aerial routes, through drones, and autonomous ground routes, through walking robots. In case you are thinking this belongs to some far future, think again. The trend has already begun, and it is here to stay and grow. Companies such as Alphabet (Wing), Amazon (Amazon Air), and DHL (DHL Parelcopter) have been already trying out robotic delivery.

Green Ships

With our roadways going green with electric cars, railways with low-pressure tube-pods, and airways with electric drones, our waterways are under equal pressure to go green, too. The journey in the water was always green at least in the past. People used muscle and wind power before the industrial revolution started ferrying people and goods from one to another location. There are multiple concepts being developed to use a combination of solar and wind power to move ships in the sea. It's not just the source of energy that's pertinent, however. Reduction of waste to aim for circular economy, which includes reduction of food waste, recycling of water, and using electric shore power, among others, are also a part of it. Carnival, one of the largest cruise companies, announced they will endeavor to achieve net carbon neutral operations by 2050. This is something less people have paid attention to but something that has more potential to transform the waterways.

How does it affect the decisions you make?

We will all be beneficiaries of the fast and revolutionary travel and transportation methods that are brewing. So, at a minimum, be in the know of these changes so you don't have to panic when you get impacted. Likewise, it's safe and smart to buy an electric car if you're looking to buy one. One that drives itself will be better even if you don't intend to let it drive. Because when the technology matures fully, you'll be one of the few who understands the business of it. If you are in the travel and hospitality industry, embracing the smart such as smart tourism and autonomous methods sooner or later pays off, keeps you afloat in the callous world of competition. Remember, if you don't learn to sail these tech waves, they will crush you. Finally, are you an entrepreneur or an investor? This field gives you enormous investment potential. Look for the trends and ensure your investments are in line with the upcoming trends. A simple thumb rule—do not put your time and money on any company that doesn't keep up with the latest trends in this industry that are predominantly driven by the latest technology.

Future of Health Care

Let's start this section in an exotic place, the Caribbean. As I utter this name, do turquoise waters and the white sand beaches come to your mind? You have every right to, but we will be going deep underwater, almost to the ocean floor, to meet *Turritopsis dohrnii*, the immortal jelly fish. Let's call her Terri. Terri loves to swim free and devour on microscopic animals attached to the submerged water plants.

She's old, weak, and fragile and cannot continue like that anymore. Rejuvenating her entire cells, Terri transforms into a younger self. In fact, she's not just transformed herself into a new self but hundreds of other Terris like her, forming a colony.

Regardless of the process, the key takeaway from this story is that Terri can transform into a younger form. She can die of other reasons, but she doesn't die of aging.

How often do you wish you could transform into a kid? Wouldn't that be amazing if humans could mimic Terri? That would be a dream come true for all of us.

The Greenland shark, *Somniosus microcephalus*, on the other hand, is not immortal, but is still a kid at 150 years (let's call him Somni). Somni can live five times the age of the longest living person on earth.

If some living being can exhibit such behaviors, why not humans, given we are the most superior species on the planet Earth (by our standard). Is there any work happening to improve life expectancy? If so, what are they? Does medical science aim at increasing life span or improving life quality or both? What can advancements in this field get us in the future, other than, of course, curing illnesses or preventing them?

While technology has been transforming every industry imaginable, it's not an understatement to say that health care is the most impacted area, in a positive way. That's because health is the most valuable property of all we possess. Given its significance, most of the complex technologies take shape in the health care industry or are at least first implemented here before making their way into other areas. For example, take the brain–computer interface and its use in the health care industry.

This is the reason this book has been soaked with discussions around the most important aspect of our lives, starting right from the tale of Falcon. Talking t-shirts, smart medicines, magic cells—we've discussed a few. I will use this section to bring all the discussions we have had on this topic into a perspective, along with anything that was left out.

A Brief History of Health Care

Health care has been in existence since the birth of humans, in some form or the other. While primitive in nature and diversified in practice, the mode of delivering this service varied depending on the culture and available resources. Health care predominantly depended on nature for managing ailments, although predominantly in the hands of God, for the longest of the times. The hunter-gatherers and agricultural societies practiced this form of treatment for centuries.

Let's take a short trip through the most documented historical lane. The 14th and 15th centuries were rocked by Black Death, also known as plague. Plague, a respiratory disease like COVID-19, also spreads through airborne droplets and is said to have killed 35 to 40 percent of the population in the United Kingdom. People thought it was coming out of thin air and attributed it to God's wrath. The worst part of it was no one knew how to prevent or cure it. Parallel to it, people died of various other diseases such as smallpox, whooping cough, measles, tuberculosis, influenza, and stomach infections in different times of history.

The average life span of the 17th-century American was around 35 years. In fact, the Americas and Europe did better than the rest of the world, with the average in Africa in the mid to high 20s. Think about it. If I belonged to the 16th or 17th century, I would be writing this book from my grave! A little further in history, the life expectancy in the late 14th century Europe was just under 20 years, although this particular dip was attributed to the spread of the plague. Compare that to today's average life span in the United States: 79 years. Average life expectancy has increased fourfold. This improvement is a direct result of advancements in science and technology.

It was only after a major breakthrough in the form of vaccines—in the late 18th century to combat some of the deadliest diseases—that wiping out diseases, such as smallpox, became possible. Vaccines gave humans additional years of cherished life on earth. Today, we rely heavily on vaccines to prevent diseases that were once thought to be insurmountable. That was only a few centuries ago. Compare that to the total life span of *Homo sapiens* on planet Earth. A major fraction of our life was spent at the mercy of God until we invented this preventive miracle.

When surgeries came around, they were tortures as much as cures. They used to be performed without any anesthesia back then, forcing a lot of people to choose death over surgery. In the mid-19th century, the surgery revolution came in the form of ether as general anesthesia although this field went through some bumpy roads where anesthesia was considered riskier than some of the surgeries themselves. However, the technology for the use of anesthesia ripened gradually. Today, we worry very little about losing lives to anesthesia. Again, this major breakthrough is only a few centuries young.

Thanks to developments in microbiology, we discovered, in the 19th century, that diseases didn't come out of thin air; they were caused by microscopic organisms. That helped us develop antibiotics and anti-viral drugs to cure ailments once thought incurable, revolutionizing medical science. Thanks to medical imaging techniques, such as X-ray, in the late 19th century and later-evolved 20th century technology magnetic resonance image (MRI)—it was finally possible to see through our bodies without peeling the flesh off and sawing the bones. Then came along organ transplants. Patients with defective organs could finally change them, saving lives of millions. If I haven't stressed enough, vaccines, drugs, diagnostics, and surgeries are all developed only within the last few centuries.

Innovation led to more innovation, and these medical inventions continued to grow throughout the industrial revolution, accelerated by the growth of large-scale organizations. However, health care industry grew to an entirely new level during the information society, with digital access to all the health care data, including that of the patient's. This access to valuable data types, for example, medical history that allowed health care providers to provide a better care, forums for providers to share their knowledge and collectively provide superior care, organized data and AI-related tools for research to come up better inventions, data-driven preventive care, and integrated information for health insurance and care providers to help patients get preventive care in order to avoid high patient care efforts, revolutionized the game. Information revolution together with technologies, such as IoT, gave rise to fitness trackers. These devices generated enormous amount of information that were processed collectively to identify risks in a larger population. Thanks to general availability of the Internet, the concept of tele-doctors and video visits have been on the rise. That's where we are now. With this in mind, what do you think our health care will look like in the future?

Role of Intelligent Technologies

Back in the Falcon's tale, we learned how AI will be used in patient care to provide an integrated health care experience to all of us. If you forgot, the summary of it was: patient data generated from various smart things around us (not just trackers) along with data from office visits and laboratories will be stored and analyzed to provide the care we require, most importantly preventive care. AI will be widely used across all the health care industry subsectors to increase efficiencies. The concept of tele-doctors and AI doctors will grow. For example, AI with access to all your data will perform initial diagnosis, often better than a physical doctor. That diagnosis may be sent to the doctor for final verification. Robots will play a major role in facilities across the health care industry, replacing humans in some cases. Robotic surgery is a great example. They perform certain operations with more precision than humans. Health care-related transport will become automated and autonomous. We will see the merge of health care and technology across all sectors of health care like never before.

Focus on Regenerative Health Care

What do we do if we have fever? We take fever suppressant. What do we do if we have pain in a body part? We take pain killers, right? A vast portion of our health care so far focused on managing the symptoms, not necessarily curing the problem. Where we do cure the issue, we do it through chemical-based medicine. The new trend in the health care industry is to use our body's ability to fight against diseases, or even cure itself, because our body does possess enormous potential to fight pathogens and survive in this complex world. That's where biotechnology comes in. The key contributors to this are stem cell therapies and genome editing.

Xenobots

Sure—you've read about robots, virtual bots, and nanobots. But what is this xenobot?

First, let me ask you a question. Can you single out a thing organic matter can offer that silicon matter cannot? The possibility of sheltering living beings inside, isn't it? Further, organic matter is biodegradable and thus is green. What if we can create nanobots that can travel to specific parts of our body, programmed to execute specific tasks, such as delivering medication, fighting cancer cells, or cleaning the plaque from the arteries? It sounds like an end-all, be-all solution to these problems, but these bots made of metal or plastic pose risks to the body. Our body is naturally resistant to foreign matter, not ready to host plastic or metal with open hands. What is the solution? We need to make these nanobots using organic material, a.k.a. the cells.

Scientists at the University of Vermont did exactly this in 2020. They took the cells from the embryos of a frog species and created new organisms through their stem cells. They used a cluster of two types of cells—one that moved and the other that didn't. Moving cells, you may ask. Yes, the heart cell. It contracts and expands to pump blood, right? Those cells were used to create motion, similar to what a motor would create, but obviously a slower one. A bunch of these heart cells and skin cells were arranged in an optimal fashion to form a new living organism that could swim using the heart muscle cells and carry small loads, such as medicine, through a hole in their structure.

This is not reprogramming the DNA of any existing species. This is not the creation of a metallic robot. And this is not the regeneration of cells in our body. If you look at it, this is the creation of a new species altogether. A living organism. Isn't that amazing? This organism is said to have enough protein inside to survive for a week. However, in a protein-rich environment, it's said to last longer, similar to any other living being. More good news, the organic bot can heal itself if damaged. And once it's dead, it is a bunch of dead cells ready to be excreted out, like so many dead cells living beings flush every day.

As simple as it sounds, the creation of this organic bot is tedious in reality. The "optimal" arrangement of cells is where the key lies. The cells can be arranged in many different combinations, as you can imagine. This is where advanced artificial intelligence came in handy. Using a super-computer called Deep Green, scientists tweaked these arrangements in a simulated environment using advanced machine learning algorithms, before they created the actual bot.

Focus on Health Span

How do we measure the quality of our health care system? In the past, we wrongly measured it through life span, meaning how long we live (right-fully so because the average life span was short in the past). We made a reasonable progress in improving our life span, although we have more work to do. But how successful are we in living the life as a free being?

A diabetic patient cannot eat his likes without having to worry about shooting up his blood sugar levels. A heart patient controls his emotion and suffers every day. Cancer patients go through those painful chemo-therapies. Improved cognition capabilities should help do things without assistance in those impacted. The point is quality of life should drastically improve or remain constant no matter what disease you have. This will be the key focus in the future.

How do we do it? It's going to be a combination of techniques. One key technique is stem cell therapy we referenced earlier. The use of AI to provide better health insights will help us mitigate any health risks before they turn into untreatable statistics. The advanced gene sequenc-ing techniques that helped us develop tools, such as mRNA vaccines, are another set of tools in our toolbox. Smart toilets we discussed that would help us diagnose health problems early on are another tool. Smart tablets we have seen in the previous chapter to diagnose health issues are another. Potential use of nanobots and xenobots that can traverse inside our bodies and target specific areas to repair cells could be another tool. While we will use various approaches to deal with this, here is the gist of our focus areas: (1) use technology to help us lead healthy lives to avoid chances of getting sick; (2) identify any health risks as early as possi-ble to mitigate them before we fall sick; (3) take preventive measures proactively, such as manufacturing and using vaccines by advanced biotechnologies; and (4) in case we fall sick, use our bodies' natural ability to cure through regenerative medicine instead of simply treating or suppressing symptoms.

Increasing Life Span

Let's revisit one of the questions we raised at the beginning of this chapter: is it possible to expand our life span? If so, how? Everything we discussed thus far is predominantly geared toward improving the quality of our life, although the indirect impact is expansion of our life span. For example, stem cell therapy's goal is to cure diseases to improve living conditions or cure deadly diseases, expanding the life span.

Generic engineering acts as a rescue mission to cure such deadly diseases. For example, the COVID-19 pandemic alone has declined the average life expectancy in the United States by a full year just in the first half of 2020. The vaccine will surely improve the average life expectancy in the future—another example of biotech improving our life span. Gene modification is showing promising results in curing genetic diseases, not just to improve the quality of life but also to help those impacted live longer. The potential use of these bio-bots we saw earlier includes the treatment of deadly diseases, resulting in a life span increase.

However, these are the technologies helping the ones impacted by diseases. Is there anything available for the healthy as well? Genetic engineering may be used one day to change our source code to slow the growth so that we can live longer, similar to those Greenland sharks. Even better, what if we figure out a way to keep converting our cells back to its younger form on par with the immortal jellyfish cells?

Instead of talking about something we haven't figured out yet, let us discuss what is possible with today's technology and what may be coming in the near future. Here's a story. When I was a kid, my dad bought a motorcycle. He used it so often it lasted for decades up until I was much older. One of my uncles bought the same model around the same time, but that only lasted a few years. Of the two motorcycles coming from the same factory around the same time as the other, ours almost lasted twice longer. Why? Because my dad took very good care of his. He maintained it periodically, replaced the parts that needed attention before they broke down, and gave it the attention it demanded.

What if we apply the same method to our bodies? Sure, we need to take care of our bodies through a healthy lifestyle, which surely does have an impact on our life span. Preventive care in terms of periodic checkups to identify risks before they become issues and mitigating them is certainly a game-changer. But what is new here? Back to the motorcycle example: my dad didn't just drive it safe, keep it clean, and feed it with good quality gasoline, but he regularly got it serviced. He replaced the old and worn-out parts.

What if we do something similar to our bodies to reverse aging? Periodically rejuvenate deteriorating or dead cells. Can proactive stem cell therapy come in handy? Perhaps. Maintain the rusting parts of the body through the removal of plaque. Can bio-bots and xenobots be employed in such a task? Such techniques, together with a healthy lifestyle, preventive care, and the advances in biotech and medicine, certainly can give us the hope of a much longer life and quality living.

Is Immortality Possible?

Man is a mortal being. Will this statement be forever true? Can we prove it wrong apart from the fact that it already is—in terms of its patriarchal tone. Anyway, who doesn't want to be immortal, right? We keep coming across several tales about immortal human beings. Various wealthy folks have taken drastic measures to improve their life spans or gain some kind of immortality; however, all of them have failed so far.

Before we get to immortality, let's quickly discuss rebirth. Rebirth is when a dead being is born again in another or similar somatic form. The *Bible* tells us that Jesus was reborn after three days. But can humans? No, I am not referring to the rebirth of a patient who died of cardiac arrest and was revived through CPR. And it's not about the repair of a failed organ within a certain time after death. Rather, I am referring to preserving the body for what lies in the future through a process called cryogenic freezing. This is the process of freezing the human body upon death for possible future resurrection, especially in a future where medical technology would have advanced to either cure the underlying cause of death or reverse aging.

There are a few companies that offer this kind of freezing. However, no frozen human has been revived so far, and this is as of today nothing more than an airy science fiction. To put this in different terms, this is based on hope or belief, and belief is often not a strategy.

If such a rebirth is just hope, is there an option backed by science?

Let me ask you a question. What makes you, you? Your skin? Your heart? Any other organ? Your brain? Of course, your brain is the one that gives you the personality you possess, defines your thought process, dictates your actions, and makes you the person you are. That's why some people with head injuries lose their memories and start their life over. Meaning, they are not the same person any longer. What if we are able to export the contents of the brain and import them into a younger body? Would that reverse aging? In a way, yes. We will look different, but our thoughts and personality will live until the new body expires. We can then import them onto a new body, as long as we find a "donee." First of all, is this mind export and import even possible? I wouldn't say it's possible yet, but thanks to the brain-chip technology (we reviewed in the previous chapter), it is plausible.

We are still in the territory of extending our life span through this complicated process with many practical challenges. I thought I said I would show you a path to immortality. Just imagine uploading your brain onto a robot, let's call it Canopus. What is the result? You made your immortal robotic twin. This is what we discussed in the last chapter. What if we create the body of a humanoid robot made from this biological wetware instead of metal? The year 2020 produced these organic nanobots that could clean up radioactive waste, collect microplastics in the oceans, carry medicine inside human bodies, and even travel into our arteries to scrape out plaque. What lies in 2030? And what will 2040, 2050, and 2060 produce? Scientists already prove that they can grow organs in a dish. What if we can put everything together and create a new regular-sized species instead of these nano-beings? Would that change everything?

We can keep the biological matter used on the lower end by only using it for skin, for example. The shell of the robot will look like a human, but it's a machine inside. We can also go right into the wetware spectrum and use body parts made of biological matter. We can model some organs as well, which are essential to keep the skin alive. But what if we could pick and choose the parts we wish to keep organic and nonorganic? The brain, the most advanced part, cannot be any lesser than an advanced AI-based computer, either complex systems of neuronal networks or biological matter. If we carefully put everything together, can we technically create a hybrid that looks like a human with the powers of a supercomputer? It sure sounds scary. Is it possible with today's technology? No. Is it plausible? Yes.

Future of Connectivity

As social beings, we are constantly in a need to connect with others. The entire human history can be summarized as an attempt to connect themselves, to transform river-dwelling primitive beings into office-going sophisticated commuters. In recent years, we have also been sharing our world with machines. For bad or for good, we have shared an umbilical cord connection with the inanimate objects as well who might know more about us than we've realized.

Connectivity outside of normal human interaction during the hunter-gatherer times was almost nonexistent. Interaction, too, was limited because of separateness. Society 2.0 brought people closer together, hence improved connectivity through social gatherings. But that was pretty much it. Apart from food production, ritual and other social gatherings, and being in a family, there wasn't much to do together. Connecting with other human beings remained a priority, however. Although nascent in nature, human connectivity started in Society 2.0 and continued into 3.0.

One of the prominent inventions of the industrial era was a telegraph, which evolved into a telephone. People could transmit their voice to far-off distance in real time through long cables and converse with other people. The invention of the Internet, being married to the telephone, initially depended on these lines to send data back and forth. The dial-up Internet, as it was called, was a technology the younger generations aren't familiar with. With a fraction-of-a-second patience and a passion for fast-life, there was no way they would have tolerated those high-pitched, rumbling dial tones.

Then, in the 1990s, came its big brother, the DSL, Internet connectivity that used the same phone lines but with a different frequency, thus avoiding interference with the voice. This discrete functionality allowed people to talk and browse Internet at the same time. It felt fascinating to not be interrupted while browsing. Further, an upgrade to dial-up system was cable-based Internet, which carried signals through copper wires. Sadly, this wasn't an efficient way to transfer the zeroes and ones as the data loss was high. Only with the advent of the permeating optical fiber cables that used light signals to transfer packets of data was lossless data transfer possible. This was a new infrastructure, providing us with speeds up to 2,000 Mbps (2 Gbps). Compare that to around 100 Mbps for DSL and around 50 Kbps (not Mbps) for dial-up; 2 Gbps is 2,000,000 times faster than 50 Kbps, fast enough for most of the world's commercial and domestic usage.

However, there was too much dependency on a cable. First, this cable infrastructure is not easy to install. You need to run these cables under the ground and sea to connect around every corner. Second, you need to be home to be able to get connected. Internet was easily accessible at home but anywhere outside was equally difficult. Despite many public places offering Wi-Fi, it was still difficult to check e-mails when you were on the go. Second, what if you are not in a public place offering the Internet?

Ever since the invention of telephone, we had a desire to cut the cord. Who wants to sit at home in one spot, glue that landline to our ear, and talk for hours, right? The invention of cordless phones didn't take us too far, both literally and metaphorically, from our home. The cellular networks available in the 1980s that allowed us to take our phone wherever we went did make us free but not for long. The battery was weak and the phone itself was bulky. Worst of all, the call quality was mediocre. But it was exciting to have a roaming phone, for the first time. That cellular network was 1G—the first generation. It only supported voice.

The second generation called 2G connectivity came in the 1990s. It was a major upgrade from 1G and supported text transfer through SMS messages (the same ones we still use to date) and even picture messages in the form of MMS.

The first decade in the 21st century gave rise to 3G, which was a phenomenal upgrade from previous 2G, providing Internet at speeds of around 3 Mbps. 3G was the reason why we could start using social media and other applications, to the point of getting addicted to them. No modern applications such as high-speed streaming and gaming would have developed, had Internet not been that faster.

The second decade of the 21st century gave us 4G connectivity, which was again a significant jump compared to 3G, offering speeds of up to 300 Mbps, paving way for HD streaming. 4G not only increased speed compared to 3G as many as 14 times, but it also reduced latency, increasing reliability on the Internet. How often do you turn off your phone's Wi-Fi to connect to 4G because of spotty Wi-Fi signals? I do that more often than I want to. That's what these G's are all about: a reliable Internet connection, often better than Wi-Fi.

3G has significantly increased outreach in underdeveloped countries, most of which depended on 2G or went without connectivity. Let's say the entire world will slowly get onto 4G. That may bring social media and digital media to everyone's phones, but will that meet our connectivity needs? To answer that question, it's essential to understand what our current and, most importantly, our upcoming connectivity needs are.

The most critical need for Internet is coming from machines, not people. And this need will grow exponentially with the number of these connected machines multiplying. Let's take the example of autonomous cars. The car must always be connected to the Internet to work effectively, not just to process tons of data it receives per second, but to know the whereabouts of all the other cars and things on the road. The future self-driving cars will speak to other vehicles on the road directly to coordinate better. They will know exactly where the traffic lights are and whether they are red, yellow, or green not by "looking at" them but because traffic lights told the cars directly through their connectivity. This level of complex coordination requires clear and uninterrupted communication between all the vehicles on our roadways and this requires a super-reliable connection.

Self-driving cars are just an example. We have already discussed that interconnected smart things will be the backbone of any smart home or a smart factory. The question is how will they talk to each other? Connectivity through cable-based Internet is difficult and even impossible for some smart things, for example, a moving car. Meeting the connectivity thirst of all the machines makes the case for a superfast, always-available wireless connection. However, more important than speed are reliability and latency. Imagine a sensor detecting potential breakdown of a gas pipe but unable to communicate to the server instantly? Such a system is practically worthless.

What is the solution? Is there a magic bullet that will get us there? These are some of the technologies I believe will dominate the scaffolding of future connectivity:

5G Availability Will Grow

If you follow the news, chances are you've heard about 5G connectivity. I hope this did not happen in the context of conspiracy theories floating around on the social media—that 5G can cause cancer or that it helped spread the COVID-19 pandemic.

5G has begun rolling out already. New devices that come to the market will be made to support this new type of connectivity. With the introduction of 5G, a big question rises in most people's minds: what will happen to 4G? Will that be replaced? Will I be forced to upgrade my cell phone to the one that supports 5G? Not so soon. With the cost and complicated setup of 5G architecture, it is likely that 4G and 5G will coexist for a long time.

If we look at the past, we had a new G almost every decade. What if I tell you that 6G is already being designed? A few 6G summits have already occurred to join forces to develop the next-next generation connectivity. Will there be 7G after that, followed by 8G?

Cell Towers Everywhere

The biggest challenge for 5G connectivity has to do with cell towers located at short distances and obstacles blocking the waves. If 5G is already facing such challenges, the future Gs either will have to completely rethink their mechanical and software infrastructure or give in to another better technology such as satellite communication, out of irrelevance and competition. Likewise, relying on cell towers installed and managed by the cell phone providers will not give us the connectivity we need in the future.

If so, what is the solution? We will have to start turning a lot of day-to-day things into cell towers. For beginners, how about our cell phones both receiving and transmitting data from and to fellow users providing connectivity to other connectivity-hungry substructures around them? How about our future furniture coming with embedded transmitters? Public infrastructure with embedded cell towers? How about partnering with the utility company to attach cell towers to electric poles? Only need will pave the path to solution. If terrestrial G-technologies survive and cellphones capable of receiving and transmitting satellite signals do not become ubiquitous, at least for 6G connectivity, it may apply all or some of the above. This space is worth examining because it is something that implicates directly to the end users, both you and me.

Connecting to the Space

I jumped the gun a little bit on this subject and introduced this in the previous chapter. As we discussed, SpaceX and Amazon are working tirelessly to provide reliable Internet connectivity through thousands of orbiting satellites to every corner of the world. This is a different form of connectivity that relies on thousands of satellites orbiting our planet instead of connectivity through terrestrial cellular towers: any G-generation, cable-based, optical, or wireless Internet connectivity.

Connected Sidewalk Through Sidewalk

Let the creator explain. According to Amazon,

> Amazon Sidewalk is a shared network that helps devices like Amazon Echo devices, Ring Security Cams, outdoor lights, motion sensors, and tile trackers work better at home and beyond the front door…When enabled, Sidewalk can unlock unique benefits for your device, support other Sidewalk devices in your community, and even locate pets or lost items. (2022)

Amazon Sidewalk creates a low-bandwidth network with the help of Sidewalk Bridge devices including select Echo and Ring devices.

These bridge devices share a small portion of your Internet bandwidth, pooled together to provide these services to you and your neighbors. And when more neighbors participate, the network becomes even stronger. The idea is to offer one more medium to enable reliable and instant connectivity demanded by all the "things" that rely on connectivity, especially not so hungry consumers, such as trackers. When the Internet connection is on, they'll use it. And technologies like Sidewalk can act as a fallback option. This has already been rolled out. If you own an Echo or a Ring, chances are you are a part of this program already or at least you have the option to participate. You can always opt out of Sidewalk if you think it follows you.

Direct Connectivity

Not too long ago, Internet was a thing only connected to computers and lately to cellphones. With the advent of LAN-enabled appliances, devices such as printers, desktops, and TVs could grow their reach and possibilities. I remember having to place my TV next to the router to avoid running a long LAN cable to connect my TV to the Internet. When I relocated the Wi-Fi router, I had to take my TV along with it as it connected only through a LAN cable. Years later, the wireless adapter came to my rescue and cut the umbilical cord between my TV and router. Everything has gone wireless today: wireless TVs, wireless ACs, wireless laptops, wireless alarm clocks, wireless headphones, and even wireless electricity. How will this connectivity work in the future? With all the advances in XG and satellite Internet connectivity, future "things" will no longer depend on a Wi-Fi connection. Instead, they will be able to connect directly to the Internet. Perhaps they will also act as transmitters as we discussed earlier to support future-generation XG connectivity.

Will all this technological gimmicks, an important question is whether cable-based Internet will fade away. Not in the near future, as far as I can tell, because of their dedicated, fast transfer of data without connectivity problems. XG, cable-based Internet, satellite Internet, and other advances such as Amazon Sidewalk will work together to meet connectivity needs of our futuristic world. But whether a technology will vanish also comes down to the service Internet companies provide us, given this tough competition between multiple sources of connectivity. You, as an end user, however, should look for two things: reliable, fast connection and affordable cost. And when there is tough competition between corporates, there is always one winner: you, the end user.

Future of Metals and Resources

What comes to your mind when you think of mining? Hard hats, dirty clothes, and dangerous working conditions? These days, you don't have to wear a hard hat, cover yourself in a protective suit, and work in dangerous, hard-to-reach underground tunnels and scariest labyrinthine ducts. You simply sit behind a computer and mine millions of dollars' worth of products that are in hot demand all over the world. Even better, you don't even have to sit behind a computer. You simply teach the computer to mine; you go and play your favorite game while the computer mines for you autonomously.

Does it sound like crypto mining? That is not the mining we talk about in this section. We are going to discuss the least attractive industry that gives the most valuable returns for humanity—mining minerals.

Two essential substances, metals and nonmetals form the major portion of both our living and nonliving worlds. Among them, the sturdy, malleable, ductile, and sonorous pieces of moldable metals are so pervasive you'll find them almost everywhere—from airplanes to electrical appliances.

Around 95 of the 118 elements in the periodic table—a table where all discovered elements are arranged systematically—are metals. Along with coal, metals and other nonmetals form the interior of the earth called minerals. Our ancestors carved the earth's minerals and resources such as stones, bones, and teeth into weapons and tools and used them to build homes and ward off wild animals.

Most metals aren't found in pure state. They compound with other substances. Mining enriches the concentration of metals from these substances. Mining of minerals to hoard metals started in the agricultural society with evidence of metals such as iron, bronze, gold, and silver extracted with great industrial fervor. In fact, these resources are so important in our life that our predocumented history is categorized by these metals (or lack thereof). Hunter-gatherer society was called the Stone Age; the early part of the agricultural society was known as the Iron Age, then followed by the Bronze Age, named after the most common sources used for daily tools and structures. Metals were used as the means of exchanging value (money) up until a few decades ago.

While mining existed for thousands of years, it definitely took a turn in the industrial society. The exponential growth in manufacturing equally grew the demand for metals that needed to be mined. The first industrial revolution brought in demand for new types of materials to be mined from the earth's core—such as coal. The second industrial revolution, the electricity revolution, fueled the need to exploit the ductile property of metals and thereby produce long wires to distribute energy to far off places. In turn, the demand for metals such as copper went up. Development of new manufacturing and construction techniques further fueled the demand for all types of metals. And the third industrial revolution, the information revolution, only grew the demand for mining, as none of the present-day electronics could be imagined without mining minerals.

With this historic growth in the mining industry, we are entering the digital industry revolution, a.k.a. Society 5.0, where the demand will only continue to grow. More economies around the globe swayed by the increasing population are graduating to better societies, using modern construction methods and manufacturing techniques. Equally, the electronics revolution has entered from affluent bungalows to impoverished huts, thanks to bettered economic conditions, with far and away declining prices. Modern-day electronics and appliances are on an all-time high manufacturing demand producing an e-waste of about 54 million tons alone in 2019; all of them rely heavily on minerals mined from the earth such as copper, nickel, cobalt, iron, zinc, aluminum, and even rare earth metals. Add to that the advances in the field of intelligent technologies we have been discussing, the hunger for mineral-made items: computers, sensors, robots, cameras, drones, weapons, tools, and everything else will only grow in the next generation's connected society.

Mine Your Business

The exponential growth in demand for specific metals such as copper and nickel driven by the "G" of the BIG future, that is, Green Technologies, will add to the total growth. An average of five times more copper is used in renewable energy sources, compared to traditional fossil fuels. An electric vehicle uses over 80 kilograms of copper and a single wind turbine uses an estimated 1900 pounds. Global wind turbine fleet is estimated to consume over 5.5 metric tons of copper by 2028 according to a 2020 report by mining.com (2019). The news extracts next should give you an indication of how the demand for mining products will grow.

"Copper is 'the new oil' and low inventories could push it to $20,000 per ton, analysts say"—by CNBC (Smith 2021).

"Green copper demand to average 13 percent annual growth over next 10 years—report," mining.com reported (2021).

Another praise for another metal: "Nickel Soars and Could Keep Flying as Demand Rises and Supply Falls," Tim Treadgold writes in the *Forbes* (2019). The article further states that the strong demand for stainless steel and supply shortages caused "the great nickel rush of 2007" hitting a record price of $50,000/t. "This time around, nickel has a new price driver, EVs, a mode of transport which was not even a blip on commodity investors radar screens in 2007," Tim further writes.

Another mining.com report says: "Cobalt demand from battery industry expected to grow in the next five years" (2020). The article cites battery technology as the primary driver for growth in cobalt mining.

"Gold Is Hot but Nickel Is Hotter as Demand Grows for Batteries in Electric Vehicles," Forbes reports (Treadgold 2019).

Mining industry is the biggest contributor to the green revolution, unlike what most people think.

While these paint a very rosy future for mining, the growth in demand doesn't apply to everything we mine. After all, mining is a very broad industry contributing to around 7 percent of the global GDP. With the global push to going green, the demand for coal will diminish even though not uniformly around the world. Some countries such as India and China may show reverse trends at least for some time but it's certain that no country can cling to fossil fuels for long.

The future-proof optimism for the mining sectors comes along a number of challenges. The first challenge will be to keep up with the demand despite its deprecating environmental repercussions. It's not that we have unlimited amounts of minerals hidden under the earth. There have been several predictions around when we will run out of various natural resources. While the jury is still out on any specific estimates, we will definitely run out of anything that is not infinite. Even if we have more minerals available somewhere in the world, we need to find new sites where these minerals can be extracted out of. Starting up a new mine is an expensive affair. Accurate mapping technologies must be developed to precisely discover these potential mines.

On the other hand, mining has its own perils with concern over the safety of miners, given it's often done underground with limited ventilation at times. Thirty-three miners were trapped 2,300 feet under the ground in Chile in 2010 for 69 days—stories as such intensify the dread. While the present-day mining safety procedures may have been enhanced, in the past there was no guarantee that people going underground would come back. It's not just the immediate safety but the working conditions that pose long-term health risks to the miners. For example, coal miners run the risk of black lung disease from the coal dust they inhale.

While the future might bring along so much opportunity in the manual mining industry, it is going to be equally threatened by other sources. Rapid advances in technology are inventing new production methods that use different types of minerals. Billionaire Elon Musk expressed concerns over nickel being the "biggest concern for scaling" the production of Li-ion batteries, through a tweet (Musk 2021): "That's why we are shifting standard range cars to an iron cathode. Plenty of iron (and lithium)!"

Advanced AI and robotics technologies might be a part of the solution: they may find new minerals inside of the earth's core, or in space, as well. What does this mean? Mining industry must not only keep up with the demand but give opportunities to look for newer methods, too. This explains how both mining and consumption markets have to keep track of each other's inherent capabilities. In addition, mining companies must also keep their research and development going to drive the change in market demands, instead of being driven, and even worse, getting disrupted.

Attracting talent has been a major challenge for the mining industry. Mining is a dangerous job and obviously one of the dirtiest. Cyber security continues to be a threat to all the mines. A single attack can bring all mining activities to a grinding halt.

With tremendous opportunities, yet more than a handful of challenges, how will mining shape up in the future? Let's look at the key trends. Again, these are generic and as with any industry we discussed thus far, specifics will vary for particular sectors within mining industry. In addition, every company is different with unique set of challenges and opportunities.

Robots All Over

Unlike humans, robots are indefatigable. They are not scared of depths and dangerous work environments, can be repaired if damaged, or simply replaced. They are emotionless, demand no rights, and are not affected by any long-term health risks. And most importantly, robots are often more effective than humans, in performing laborious as well as intelligent tasks. That way, robots would be more suited to mining work than humans. And that's exactly what is going to happen. From ore prospecting to actual mining, mineral extraction, smelting, processing, and transportation, autonomous robots can play a vital role. Part of these functions are already automated in several mines across the globe.

Note that robot is a pretty broad term and consists of various types ranging from drones, drilling bots, and other mining machinery all the way to autonomous vehicles. These robots, powered by advanced AI, will perform almost at the capacity of this fictitious super humans from sci-fi movies, that too, 24/7.

A news reports that exclaims "Robots are replacing humans in the world's mines" further writes in the byline: "One day the world's mines may be operated almost entirely by machines" (Baggaley 2017). The news piece further points out it's possible that future mining might take place inside ocean floor—thanks to automation. "Making use of robots may be our only chance to ever extract minerals in such areas." Humans can opt out from doing dangerous jobs into more secure fields.

Circular Mining

Mining is generally tied to the excavation, extraction, and enrichment of natural resources pertaining to the interior of the earth. But what about the vast stretches of waste, "good-for-nothing" reserves we have on land? Circular mining addresses this very concern, making mining from recycled products possible. With the exponential growth in demand, the best way to increase supply is remine from the products that were once mined. This is a part of the circular economy.

Pretty much every mining company is deploying recycling plants and working on recycling metals. But there's more to it. Mining companies alone cannot effectively remine metals. Instead of leaving it up to everyone to initiate the recycling process by handing over their used resources, there must be a business model to enforce recycling. A subscription model to products where we pay for using the items rather than owning them so the manufacturer gets their products back at the end of their life can be one of the models to enforce recycling. This model is surely picking up steam. The manufacturing process must be accorded to make it easy to remine these metals from used products. Moving toward modular designs is one such technique.

Biomining

Extracting metals from wastes and ores is indeed a grueling task. As of late, both giant and intelligent machines are assisting in the task, but by no means have they made it as easy as the game of chess. The game of chess? Is it too much to ask for? Or can mining, or say remining, be made a laidback industry as I'm talking here.

Turns out, there's a way. Mining can be done at ease with the assistance of the armies of the nature—the tiny organisms that eat away stuff on earth. When you employ tiny organisms to mine metals from their ores and wastes, it's called biomining. *The Conversation* explains biomining as: ". . . technique promised by science fiction: a vast tank filled with microorganisms that leach metal from ore, old mobile phones and hard drives" (Voutsinos 2022). Microorganisms can feed on scrap metal parts and containers such as electronic wastes and extract precious metals such as gold, copper, nickel, zinc, and rare earth metals. It can be one of the most ecological methods to reduce both the carbon footprint and the extra burden on earth's natural reserves. Biomining is currently used to produce about 5 percent of the world's gold and 20 percent of the copper, Voutsinos says. It is a technology expected to lead to supply growth through its ability to extract metals from low-grade ores.

There are also various attempts to mine precious metals by using living cell efficiencies, such as that of a bacterium's. Labiotech, a leading digital media that covers European biotech industry, published an article "Biomining: Turning Waste Into Gold With Microbes," reporting the German technology by a company called BRAIN (Biotechnology Research and Information Network) that converts "trash to treasure" (Mitha 2022). The company reportedly employed more than 50,000 "to identify the most talented metal-extracting microbes and put them to work." These are some of the great examples of the use of biotechnology in mining.

Smart Mining

Imagine a mine packed with robots working autonomously across the entire mining supply chain. These robots generate huge amounts of data uploaded to the control center in real time. But they aren't the only machines that generate the data; a plethora of sensors embedded in the mine, inside those robots, in the smelter, and everywhere else in the supply chain continuously feed data back to the center. These sensors leverage the data from parameters such as the temperatures inside the smelters and mines to positioning of the transport vehicles and let the central station decide, and automatically, whether the temperature is beyond or under preferred values or what the status of raw materials are. Interestingly, the entire process—from ore enrichment all the way to the finished material and from mining to the delivery of the finished product—is displayed on the big screen by configuring through a digital twin. Or even better, if the engineer wants to get a more realistic, less 2D feel of things, the incorporation of virtual reality lens makes it possible for her to site-visit wherever she wants and in real time.

Virtual Mining

Where is this control center located? Outside the mine? Outside the smelter? Near the distribution center? Near the recycling plant? The choice is yours. Do you want to put this on a Caribbean beach or in an ancient quiet town of Alaska? How about a mobile control center you can simply operate from your handheld device? Nothing will stop you from doing it, if company policies allow.

The great news is you don't have to wear a hard hat, cover yourself in a protective suit, and work in dangerous underground tunnels hard to reach and breathe in. Sit behind a computer and mine those millions of dollars' worth of products that are in hot demand all over the world. Even better, you don't even have to sit behind a computer. Teach the computer to mine; you go and play your favorite game while the computer mines for you autonomously. Does this sound familiar? If not, please go back to the beginning of this section. If mining can be made so cool, would you be interested in being a part of it?

Space Mining

Natural resources are finite and there's no way of getting around them because we're isolated on a planet, millions of kilometers away from another mine-able planet. We will come up with more efficient solutions but will that be enough to meet the demand decades from now? What is our fallback option? The good news is while resources are finite on our planet Earth, there are plenty of earth-like objects in the space and the resources are almost infinite, provided we figure out a way to reach there, mine their resources, and bring them back to earth, or better, don't.

Whether we mine on other heavenly bodies and bring those resources to earth or use them to colonize space in the future, the rate at which we're exploiting the resources here on earth, it'll certainly be the only option for further getting our hands on resources. The rocket technology being developed by a number of private firms together with efforts from NASA and other space agencies around the globe is making this hypothetical situation more and more possible every day.

This snippet from NBC News from July 2019, "Mission to rare metal asteroid could spark space mining boom: Scientists think it is mostly made of nickel and iron, but could also be abundant in more valuable metals such as platinum and gold," explains a lot about our future ambitions (Chow 2019). On the side, it also indicates that we're finally acknowledging that earth's resources are limited, and the way we're eating off its resources, we'll desperately need energies from another heavenly body.

Check this out from NASA that demonstrates efforts and some progress in space mining:

> Microbes to Demonstrate Biomining of Asteroid Material Aboard Space Station…As humanity moves closer to the possibility of living and working millions of miles from Earth on planets like Mars, scientists are looking beyond our planet at how to acquire the materials needed to establish a self-sustaining presence in space. (Johnson 2020)

While space mining might sound like a laidback sophistication on surface, it is too tough to chew when it comes to cost and technology. Lifting heavy-weight equipment to space is extremely difficult, leaving us with more creative options such as biomining. I also see this as inevitable, not necessarily in years, but decades. If you have any creative ideas to help enable this, you might be the first Astrominer. Or call yourself Minonaut? The choice is yours.

Future of Electricity

We discussed many industry trends in this chapter thus far from Society 1.0 to the modern day. Electricity never existed until the industrial revolution, making this industry one of the youngest. My father studied under a candlelight and streetlight in the 1950s and 1960s in the village of Kalingapatnam, in southern India. While this remote village was one of the last ones to get electricity at a large scale, the world, including developed nations like the United States, was in a similar situation a decade or so before that. Today, electricity has reached almost all remote parts of the world, although many parts of the world still experience power shortages.

From the "war of electricity" in the late 1800s between AC and DC types to the present-day tussle between fossil fuel and renewable energy, the way electricity is produced, transmitted, distributed, and retailed—we can say that a lot of changes were brought in a short time.

Electricity production techniques have evolved and diversified through sources such as hydro, wind, solar, nuclear, and fossil fuels. Pendulum-based manual meters evolved into electric meters with remote monitoring features, then to the present-day smart meters with net metering capabilities. Grids evolved from being isolated to being interconnected. Transmission equipment in general has become smarter and safer.

However, with the ever-growing technology use, energy needs are also growing tremendously. Electricity industry in general faces several key challenges. For example, regulations change frequently. Power generation has to meet the demand in real time to eliminate waste, because the energy storage cost continues to skyrocket. Despite that, storage (battery) technologies are emerging at a faster pace, driving the need for extensive research and development as well as quick partnerships to get an edge in this area. New moving-electricity consumers are emerging along with the demand of electric vehicles making electric retail even more challenging. Similarly, transmission and distribution technologies are updating frequently as well with innovation, posing challenges to keep the assets up to date for these asset-rich organizations. Wildfires, hurricanes, and other natural calamities as always pose risk to electricity distribution equipment, causing major disruptions. Power lines in many instances have caused wildfires. Cyber-attacks on the grid continues to be a looming threat to electric companies. Ransomware attack, one of the most feared, is another challenge that causes double devastation. Likewise, majority of electricity production today is fossil fuel based, a harbinger of energy crisis not very far. With several governments putting timelines to go net zero on carbon emissions, the need for moving to renewable electricity sources, nevertheless, is growing. Likewise, customers' adoption of solar that can make them independent of the utility company (where it is legally allowed) is changing the utility companies from a utility selling company to utility servicing company, making the customers the new partners. This number is proliferating. Frequent market changes also pose significant challenges to an asset-rich electricity business. This list can go on but the key trends in electricity industry that will address these challenges can be attributed to the following.

The Bright Star in the Sky

Ten thousand times more energy than the total global use strikes earth continuously and most of it gets wasted. Solar power is expected to be a dominant source of electricity by 2030, especially in those countries that receive an abundant amount. Renewables, led by solar power, will become the major source of the world's electricity by that time, according to an analysis by International Energy Agency, ewg.org. This explains the future of electricity. If your home is not solar-powered yet, you might be missing on all the free energy that's been bestowed on the earth by the nearby star and which is guaranteed to continue at least for the next five billion or so years. You don't need to pay the sun for its light nor would you have to risk its vanquishing by other technologies. Sunlight is plenty and it can be used to power almost every aspect of our life. Your investments will not only be paid back, but will help the earth recover from the perils of nonrenewable sources.

According to a report by U.S. Energy Information Administration (EIA), renewable energy sources accounted for about only 21.5 percent of the total U.S. electricity generation in 2021 (2022). These numbers are even worse around the globe. That means a majority of electricity is "unclean." Our job is to replace nonrenewable sources with renewables, rapidly but systematically.

Microgrids

A microgrid simply is a grid at a very small scale that can run independently of the main grid. These grids generate enough power to cater to the needs of the population they serve. They can still be connected to the main grid when they need more power than they produce. These grids can power one small community, one business, or simply a single home. If we take your home as an example, imagine generating, distributing, and consuming your own electricity, essentially running your own "electricity company" that lets you disconnect from the utility company (the central grid.) That's the concept of a microgrid.

Many mistake solar panels with a microgrid that can make you independent from the utility company. Solar panels in most circumstances are connected to the main grid run by the utility company and can act as extended power generators. However, through this concept of net metering, you use the power generated and the remaining goes back into the grid moving the electric meter backwards. When the main grid goes down, you would lose power in your house, too, because the utility company doesn't want the power produced by your solar panels through the grid. Moreover, you need the central grid to power your home when you are not producing enough. You can convert your solar system into a microgrid though, thus gaining independence from the main grid. One way to do this is through home battery installation. The light charges the battery and the battery powers your house in the dark. It will also act as a wall between your home and the main grid, blocking power transfer to the grid when it's down.

However, electricity grids are prone to failures due to natural calamities, human errors, or cyber-attacks. The Pacific Southwestern blackout of 2011 for almost 12 hours forced restaurants to throw away food worth $18 million, with a total of $118 million economic losses (Showley 2011). A powerful storm in 2012 caused blackout in 11 states with some places taking 7 to 10 days to restore power. Hurricane Sandy forced some people into blackout almost for two weeks. Post hurricane Maria power outages lasted almost 11 months in Puerto Rico. The solution to these problems is a microgrid, essentially making you independent from the central power production and distribution.

Smart AI Grid Managers

These microgrids must be smart enough to efficiently channel electricity to different grids. Let's say the community you are living in runs on a microgrid. It should use its own power when the cost of electricity supplied by the utility company is high. When the rate goes down, it's best for your grid to use the electricity from the main grid and store the power it generates in that battery pack so it can be used when the main grid's rate goes up. Your grid should also read usage patterns and other planned events, forecast demand, and manage supply accordingly. For example, if the majority of homes in your community wash clothes between 9 and 11 a.m. for a few weeks, it's likely that the same pattern will repeat, and a smart grid will be prepared by storing enough power in the battery ahead of time. Your home grid can gain access to your calendar and sell the power instead of storing if you're away, maximizing the money you can make. Being back on track is not a problem; it will know when you will come back and resume usual operations because it has access to your itinerary. This won't stop here. Your home grid will monitor the power usage patterns of your appliances and tell you how to optimize the use, saving you a lot. For example, it may be best if you use high-power consuming appliances when your panels are producing optimum energy or when the main grid's power is inexpensive. Instead of taking an educated guess, your smart grid manager will give you all these insights.

Wireless Electricity

Nicola Tesla, who contributed heavily to the design of electricity supply system, originally envisioned electricity transmitted wirelessly. Electricity is transmitted through wires; we know the truth now and haven't been able to march an inch forward from that fact, with the exception of some low-energy applications. Our homes still run these wires and none of our equipment work without plugging in.

The battery came in with a big promise to "cut the cord," but still needs to be charged and most of all doesn't run AC equipment without an inverter. The one ubiquitous wireless electricity transfer method that we have been able to master is wireless battery charging. We can already buy wireless phone chargers. In a few years' time, gone will be the days when you need to sit next to a power outlet to charge your laptop or run a long extension cable to power that vacuum cleaner or install your TV next to a power outlet, although the biggest use case for wireless electricity is wireless electric vehicle charging. Charging roads through inductive charging can make that possible. It's just a matter of time that this technology will come to our homes. While these advances fall in the end-user's side of electricity, a startup called Emrod in collaboration with New Zealand government will be testing wireless power transmission over long distances through a partnership with the country's second-largest power distributor Powerco (Delbert 2021). If successful, that will be a major breakthrough toward Tesla's vision of powering cities wirelessly.

Wireless transmission, because of the same reasons, looks like a long shot at the moment; however, a lot of progress is being made in smaller scales. Wireless electricity transfer is one of the most groundbreaking patents waiting to happen, and most importantly, to materialize.

Energy Storage

The biggest challenge with electricity is that the supply has to match the demand in real time, else the rest will go waste. That's because storing electricity, especially in huge amounts, is still very expensive. This is an area rapidly improving, the growth accelerated through electric cars and other transportation options dependent on stored electricity. Being able to store the surplus kilowatts of energy for future usage also reduces our dependency on fossil fuels.

CNBC reported in an article titled "The Battery Decade: How Energy Storage Could Revolutionize Industries in the Next 10 Years" that Union Bank of Switzerland (UBS) "estimates that over the next ten years[,] the energy storage market in the United States could grow to as much as $426 billion" (Stevens 2019). Statista estimates that the global demand for batteries is expected to increase from 185 gigawatt-hours in 2020 to over 2000, by 2030 (Placek 2021). Whether we bring that much-awaited leap in energy storage technology depends on how the research on solid-state and other battery technologies unfold in the years to come. Innovators, are you listening? The opportunities are endless.

Robotic Helpers

When I was driving one fine evening, I was stopped by traffic on the street leading up to our home. An extremely tall crane carried a gentleman to the top of the electrical grid line. He tied himself to a rope and dropped down to conduct some repair on it. It looked so scary and painful, I couldn't imagine it was happening in the United States. When I reached home, I Googled the fact and was shocked to learn from U.S. Department of Energy's website (osti.gov) that working in electricity and associated fields is dangerous with an estimated 81,258 fatalities between 1969 and 2000 in the energy sector alone (Burgherr and Hirschberg 2005).

But it doesn't have to be all doom and gloom. The good news is: there are robotic helpers that can either complement humans in executing such complex tasks or replace them. It's the easiest method to bring that statistic down to zero.

Digital Twin and Predictive Analytics

Imagine a grid equipped with sensors: one sensor on every pole to detect the equipment and electricity statuses, a sensor each on transformers and other intermediator equipment, on meters to detect equipment fluctuation and failure, and along the way to detect weather conditions. The real-time sensor data along with data from smart meters are consolidated back by an AI to formulate a digital version of the grid, called a digital twin. If a sensor on a transformer detects excessive heat, the digital twin will know exactly where the problem is and most likely what it is. It will create an automatic work command, order the exact part required, and will summon the repair crew. This is how future utility companies will gain control on the grid, predict issues, and manage them proactively.

Solar Space Farm

The earth's atmosphere and surface absorbs and reflects almost 70 percent and 30 percent of solar radiation, respectively (Rhodes 2010). The idea behind a solar space farm is to harvest solar power in the space instead of on land to avoid the loss of solar energy on entry. In addition to increased radiation energy, this tapping process also results in longer collection time due to throughout-the-year sun time. Giant arrays of solar panels can be launched into space, which will orbit the earth tapping tremendous amount of solar energy. With more advances in the space technology, the cost of sending these panels can easily plummet. The only problem is sending the power back to earth. Running long electric cables from ground up would be impractical, not to mention the logistical difficulty.

How about wireless transfer? The panels can wirelessly transfer concentrated beams of high-power microwaves to earth at a particular angle that will be caught on a receiving plant and converted to electricity. At a minimum, this electricity can be used to fuel all the flying objects such as future air buses, air taxis, drones, and probably space buses. One such technology already exists today. The headline of a CNN news report reads: "A solar panel in space is collecting energy that could one day be beamed to anywhere on Earth" (Walsh 2021). "The panel—known as a Photovoltaic Radiofrequency Antenna Module (PRAM)—was first launched in May 2020, attached to the Pentagon's X-37B unmanned drone, to harness light from the sun to convert to electricity." Revolving around the earth in every 90 minutes, the drone presents itself as a working model. This technology is in its infancy, but this space is definitely worth watching.

The continuous demand for electricity presents with tremendous opportunities in terms of entrepreneurship and employment. Battery technologies, wireless distribution, smarter and safer equipment, data analysis, and distribution and consumption to build smarter AI—these are just a few spaces for entrepreneurs and futurists to watch. It goes without saying that we must go green not because doing so will deem us woke, but because we have no other choice.

Future of Entertainment

Entertainment has become so essential an aspect of our lives that it wouldn't be an overstatement to put it in the same category as food and shelter. We don't realize the importance of it to say the least. The best way to understand the importance of anything is to imagine a world without it. Imagine yourself in a room without a TV, without anyone to talk to, no book to read, and no smartphone to connect to the outside world. On the first read, this may sound great. Many of us want to take a break from our day-to-day demanding lives and hide somewhere, disconnected from the rest of the world. In that context, yes, this might be a relief for a while. But what if you could never go back to where you are now? Or you never had these tools to take a break from. Life without any means of entertainment would mean work, work, and only work without any means to de-stress and relax. Breakdowns would be more common. And people would burn out, leading to severe health issues.

Social gatherings, storytelling, music, games–these are the fundamentals of entertainment. Social gatherings are meant to promote culture, contact, and communication. Storytelling comes in mainly verbal and visual forms. Music harmonizes the soul. Games played both indoor and outdoor, single- or multiplayer, violent or nonviolent, and outcomes driven by skills, strengths, or chance, act as drills for nurturing health, association, and intellect. These fundamentals of entertainment have been the same since our early ancestors and, to nobody's wonder, might continue to be. They manifest their presence differently based on various factors such as culture, availability of resources, climate, politics, and technology.

For example, our hunter-gatherer ancestors got together, often near a fire, telling stories to each other and playing music with raw-from-nature musical instruments carved out of bird bones and ivories of large animals, such as elephants and mammoths. Games were probably athletic and striving to sharpen their survival skills and hunting confidence, such as running, striking, parrying, grappling, and/or throwing objects. Similar trends continued into the agricultural society without any significant changes, although details were driven by cultural and political influence. Gladiator games, for instance, were popular in Roman times, led by political and cultural influences. Social gatherings celebrated local cultures. Ancient Roman bath houses are an example, embellished eloquently in a unique setting, driven by Romans' desire of relaxing and socializing. The point is that entertainment options revolved around similar fundamental principles of social gatherings—storytelling, music, and games—and were modified to fit the culture, politics, and resources.

The advent of industrial society registered some notable progress in the entertainment world. Traditional skits and music were industrialized with the growth in organized plays and music shows, accelerated by the invention of microphones, speakers, and other electronics. Thanks to the advances in construction, more theaters erupted where shows were organized. Advances in transport gave access to more entertainment options located far from home. Better entertainment options were made available at night other than those done using torches and campfire, thanks to electricity and light bulbs. The art revealed itself in a myriad of ways with sophisticated musical instruments and further development in electronics industry. Without a doubt, entertainment industry started witnessing a rapid change in the industrial society. Telephones allowed social connects from the comfort of our home. Radios allowed remote broadcast of social messages, music, and stories allowing people to access them from the comfort of their homes. And finally, when transistors made radios portable and gave access to this entertainment on the go, people could take entertainment wherever they went.

However, without a doubt, one of the greatest inventions of the industrial society was not audio or musical instruments; it was the picture, specifically the motion picture. Traditional and manual skits were initially supplemented and slowly replaced by this brand-new entertainment option—in the form of "movies" people went crazy about. Theatregoing at least once in their lifetime became common. Further advances in electronics technology brought along TVs, where folk could access real, visual entertainment from home. TVs became more attractive with more channels offering a variety of entertainment options right from people's living rooms. These motion pictures eventually made their way into people's homes through their television sets. The entertainment industry has changed humanity so much with its over-the-century transformation that an alien visiting the earth before and after would certainly mistake it for another planet.

As we entered the information society, the entertainment industry continued to transform at a faster pace. Internet allowed the growth of streaming services such as Netflix. When was the last time you rented a physical DVD or even older VHS tape (if the young generation even knows what I am talking about)? Simply broadcasting on a TV or radio is not sufficient anymore. Every media company must stream their content these days. Some movies are streamed online without even a day release in theaters. COVID-19 pandemic certainly has accelerated this process with people reluctant to go to theaters.

The gaming industry went digital as well. No, I am not referring to digitally streaming physical games. Well, that's happening too. But the concept of "digital games" have picked up pace. People play with each other on the digital space now. In 2020 alone, digital gaming generated

$159.3 billion of revenue and is increasing; an expected 9.3 percent annual growth will yield a revenue of more than $200 billion in 2023 (Field Level Media 2020). And these digital games have huge audience with well-off players. Online betting is on the rise where it's allowed.

But when the game-changing invention in the information society, the social media, came about, lines were clearly drawn between entertainment and addictive industry. Big players such as Google, Facebook, Instagram, Twitter, and TikTok and other social media companies stole people's attention and glued them to their devices. These social media platforms took the social gatherings, the core aspect of entertainment, and brought it to the digital world. You can not only talk to your friends from the comfort of your couch, but you can talk to them as if real and at any time. It's amazing to feel the ability to connect to anyone in the world with a click. Talking to strangers has become easier, without the social anxiety kicking. Social media platforms are also powerful in that they give forums for everyone to share their stories, music, and videos with the rest of the world, democratizing the world of entertainment. That's the biggest disruption social media brought to the world of entertainment. Again, this decentralization of entertainment industry has groomed millions of ordinary people and given them wealth, name, and fame, without having to go through the same struggle the earlier generations did.

Arguably the biggest advancement, however, was the invention of a smartphone, which enabled access to the media content on individuals' hands. Roughly two generations back, during my grandfather's time, radios were as big as today's regular-size TVs and nonmobile; people gathered around this audio device. In my dad's generation, radio could be carried in a pant pocket in the form of a transistor. TVs were massive boxes that families befriended to. Today, TVs can be carried in our pant pockets in the form of smartphones and are capable of online streaming, gaming, socializing, entertainment, and countless other acts. Radios became portable in the previous generation. TVs became portable in this generation. What is in the store for the next generation?

While that is tough to predict, here are some of the top trends in entertainment.

The Metaverse

Parallel to the physical world resides the virtual world, complete in and on itself: called as metaverse or its ultimate superset, omniverse. These virtual worlds that either simulate the real world or new worlds on their own are already happening as of today.

Let's say you are bored of the world around you. You put on your virtual reality headset, program an alternate universe, and live in that alternate world as long as you want, thanks to virtual reality. VR technology is here to stay and grow, hence this will only get better. This technology is so powerful that you won't be able to tell the difference between a virtual and a real world, as long as you are in your VR headset (which may not be a head "set" any longer; it may be glasses or even lens). Switching between two completely different worlds will be as easy as wearing something on your head. But that's the simplistic use case for this metaverse. Movies will use this technology to truly "immerse" you into an alternate world. Gaming will take you into the gaming universe. These will not be "video" games any longer. Call them "omni world" or "meta world" games. Your workplace meetings occur by a beautiful beach with tranquil waters and soothing sounds of ocean waves, all virtually created, bringing a great element of entertainment into the work place. Some of the school field trips happen in the classroom (or even at the comfort of home) through the creation of a virtual world. How interesting would it be to go on a field trip to Mars or even into other galaxies?

Augmented Role Play

All people want to be their favorite TV or virtual character. Playing a lead character in the next blockbuster movie, playing Tom Hanks or Brad Pitt or Angelina Jolie or Jennifer Aniston, was a dream, until now.

Whoever your favorite character in a movie is, they will be replaced, not in the very far future. Who will replace them? You. Relax, you do not need to know any acting. You can act in movies as long as you know how to wear a VR headset.

How does this all work? Let me elaborate. When you are ready to watch your favorite movie, you will be given an option to pick the actors and actresses. You want to play the lead role? You simply make that choice. You will be able to pick other characters as well. The real characters in the movie will be replaced by the faces of your choice. If this sounds like a movie with faces replaced by some fake faces, think again. This experience is going to look so real that if you show this augmented role play to someone new, he would believe that you were the real actor or actress in that movie, including all the expressions. And did I mention that your voice will be used as well? Yes, the dialogue will be in your voice if you want. You may have to record your voice one time for a few seconds.

While it may not happen tomorrow, the day will come when you not only get immersed in the new virtual movie world, you can play one of the roles. I sure want to pick the role that doesn't die at the end. What would be your choice?

The Media Is the Message

Recently, the democratization of the media industry through social media platforms has increasingly raised a big question—will the conventional, organized entertainment companies such as studios and channels disappear?

The answer is, again, no.

All big players must and will adopt to the new trends even if that means a complete U-turn to their business models. YouTube certainly has its own space but it is not going to replace traditional media and entertainment companies because these media are consumed for a different purpose. Their relationship will be complimentary rather than substitutive. One of the adoptions traditional media companies must make is to include digital media platforms as a part of their going-to-the-market strategy. Let's take the example of the print media, which without a doubt got majorly impacted by the digital revolution. Did all newspapers disappear? No, they're still here and around. They adopted newer means to reach their audience. And most importantly, social media will act as the breeding ground for talent that more traditional media companies can use. That way, social media gives equal opportunities to everyone regardless of position and place, but digital media in itself will not replace traditional media companies, at least not any time soon.

Online Gaming

Online gaming will pick up more steam: gaming has always been a solid means of entertainment for ages and we already saw gaming move to the digital world through video games that eventually evolved into online and digital matches. The gap between playing games with virtual characters in a metaverse and with humans is getting slimmer day by day. But whoever the partner is, the medium has increasingly become online and digital. According to some estimates, there are currently one billion online gamers in the world and that number is expected to reach 1.3 billion in the next five years. In 2020, online gaming generated approximately U.S. $21 billion (Clement 2022). If we do a rough math to match the user projections, the revenue will pick up more steam with this industry expected to reach around U.S. $2.8 billion in the next five years. With very high level of confidence, I can tell you that this subsector within the entertainment industry will disrupt the forms of entertainment. You cannot go wrong in this: participating in this growth in whatever capacity you can, whether you want to work in this industry or invest, is a good bet.

Theatrical Sailors

It's almost certain that "streaming only" platforms will never completely do away with theaters even though it might seem likely especially during difficult times like the COVID-19 pandemic. Although they started opening up, COVID has without a doubt caused a massive damage to theater business, movie theaters, amphitheaters, and auditoriums alike. Meanwhile, people got used to watching streamed content on their televisions and handheld devices. Many speculate that this may be the beginning of theaters journey toward extinction. The best way to answer this question is to look at past trends.

Although it's not a direct comparison, let's travel back to the days the motion picture began. There were fears that theatrical drama would go out of business. Did it? Now, if we compare watching a movie at home and watching it in a theater, the experience is entirely different. That's a decision content producers will have to make and it depends on a lot of parameters. That said, theater business *will* be disrupted and theaters must become more creative. Perhaps theaters with newer concepts such as the ones that provide dining experiences. Theaters must become creative, turn into entertainment centers with more entertainment options than just a movie or a show besides expanding their footprint in people's lives. Theatre Chain Company American Multi-Cinema (AMC) decided to sell their popcorn outside of their theaters, not just to generate new revenue streams, but also to live with their customers outside of the theater.

News Authenticity

We live in a world where we suffer from information overdose. Information keeps coming to us through numerous sources. Some of them are "authentic" sources, while most are shady, fake, and manipulated. Sometimes the facts are conflicting and the story is made up. Who to trust and what to believe aren't taught in schools; this is not something that we're trained in. Should we trust messages on the social media? Should we follow more traditional outlets? Introduction of technologies like Deep Fake makes it even more difficult to trust anything we see. Social media propagandas with malicious intent have been on the rise and unfortunately have succeeded to fool people. Deep fakes can be as malevolent as a weapon of mass destruction when the technology matures. Radical political groups have pushed their propaganda and conspiracy theories to a whole new level. For those who do not have enough time or skill to delve deeper, anything they hear from a group sounds like truth. Governments around the world are using more authoritarian approaches to control the media content, and in some instances acting as the aggressor themselves. That might seem to work for a while but is undemocratic. They tend to tip the media scales into their favor. However, I believe there is a major opportunity to solve this "media authenticity" challenge throughout the world though there's not a one-shot kill cure.

There are multiple solution options here, and I think the ultimate solution, although partial, will be a combination. First, governments need to jump in and put in some controls in place. These controls will differ from country to country, but it's time some action is taken, depending on what is allowed by law. For example, free speech can be protected, but at the same time people should be held accountable for knowingly perpetuating false information. Second, private and independent groups should take up this task to ensure authenticity of the content that gets circulated. It could be one organization or a platform where common people provide a certificate of authenticity. Think of the use of blockchain technology to help enable this "certification of authenticity" of digital content. And third, people in general should take the baton against this problem and lean toward authentic outlets to get their news. Unless we include systematic methods of fact-checking in the syllabuses of schools, learning this "trivial" task of information policing is going to be harder. Regardless of how it will be done, there will be enormous emphasis on "real news" in the years to come.

4D Technology

Have you ever watched a 4D movie (as they call) that adds a "fourth dimension" to movie scenes for instance by seat movements, water sprays, and other gimmicks? This is to create an immersive experience on top of the 3D experience. That is not an easy task as it is often created specific to a movie to match specific scenes. For example, when there is a tremor, your seats vibrate to mimic that experience. However, with AI, that experience can be modularized and applied to any movie that choses to incorporate that experience. Common standards must be developed to enable this experience so there's a seamless and less cumbersome process going on in the postproduction. 4D movie-making process must embed protocols such as establishing communication between the movie and the physical infrastructure in theaters. For example, a certain command can be embedded when water is to be sprayed. The play back sends a signal to the spray system within the theaters when that command is to be executed. The same logic can apply to other scenes and situations, embedding their own unique commands. While this is complicated, this is a basic blueprint that could be developed further. I do see this as an opportunity for entrepreneurs in the media and entertainment space.

To summarize, watch out for metaverses, which are nothing but 3D extensions of the Internet on the rise. All the fundamental building blocks of entertainment, namely social interactions, gaming, and storytelling, will move to this metaverse with an emphasis on authentic content. However, traditional channels that provide real social interactions such as malls, theaters, and theme parks will, too, find their own audience. Thanks to the advances in immersive technologies, the physical world and the virtual world will beautifully work side by side to provide an ultimate entertainment depending on our interests and mood.

Future of Education

Let's start this section by taking a small field trip. Imagine you and I are visiting a factory, witnessing the massive production line. Raw material is being fed into the machinery. A product is produced at the first line; more ingredients are added to it and sent into the second where a few more ingredients are added until the product reaches the final point in the assembly line. Quality controls are put in place at every step to ensure the end product is of the best quality. The products at each step are sent to the next if they pass the quality check; if not, they are either processed back again from the beginning of the previous step, sent as by-products to manufacture something else, or simply discarded. It is remarkable to watch raw materials develop into a product, isn't it?

Now, let's go visit this animal farm next door. We enter this large farm; there are cattle and pigs, horses and sheep, in their respective sheds. We get a private tour from the cattle farmer himself who explains how the production works. These cattle are produced in batches. The young cattle are carefully followed through their life; they are treated with certain things at certain times based on their age; and the end "products" are categorized into grades. The best-grade meat goes to grade-one stores and restaurants; next-grade meat goes to the next-level stores and restaurants and so forth.

I bet you are wondering where we're getting to, when we were supposed to talk about education. Replace the factory with today's school system, the big and beautiful machinery—the classroom and kids—with the products being produced. That's today's school system. In some ways,

I find it unfortunate to compare the educational institutions with boring factories or the cruel process of animal production and many people might reject this analogy—which I respect—whether or not you agree with this.

These analogies have been drawn long ago and with magnificent clarity and this is not necessarily a wicked thing to do. Schools acted like production lines for a reason: to follow the principles of the industrial revolution and meet its demands.

Learning started as early as the evolution of life itself. Cells learned from their mistakes and perfected complex animals. Higher animals and birds learn to find prey, migrate, defend, and struggle for existence. This might sound strange because our mind has been trained to look at learning as something that requires sit-in in buildings and people vomiting knowledge onto the thirsty, the empty ones.

That's because we use learning and education interchangeably, which is a very common mistake. Learning is simply the process of knowing something new, either through education or experience.

Education doesn't have to be a formal process, either. It simply is a process where you are taught by a teacher, and a teacher can be anyone or anything. We get taught things from the day we are born, by our parents and others around us.

Our ultimate goal in life is to learn, because there are two things that never stop—learning and selling. Education is one means of learning and it is not the only means. And where does schooling fall into all this? It is but a means to dissipate education in a structured manner.

With this context setting behind us, let's take a short trip through the history of education. As with other "industries," let's start with the hunting society. There was no formal education (schooling) in this society. People learnt their skill predominantly from their ancestors, but also others in the society. All forms of education were informal.

Similar trends continued into the first part of the agricultural society. Some forms of formal schools were started later on, especially with the proliferation of civilizations. These schools were either run by the king or the religious leadership for the most part and most of them were geared to teach patriotism or faith or both. The invention of the script accelerated this schooling process, but the system was not well organized as it is today. At some point, there was a single school system where there was one school for the entire town, usually located in the middle, so everyone could walk to it. And this one school was a one-size-fits-all school. Imagine a 5- and a 15-year-old going to the same school together and studying in the same classroom. There was no formal or standard curriculum and the school decided what was worthy of teaching and what was not. Also prominent in some parts of the world, commenced mainly in Southeast Asia, were residential schools known as the *Gurukuls*, where kids lived with the guru, the teacher, for extended periods of time and learned social behavior and life skills. These are similar to the modern-day boarding schools, but without a prescribed curriculum.

The beginning of the industrial society systematized schooling. Governments started running taxpayer-funded schools but neither was it nowhere at a scale accessible for everyone, nor was the system formalized like today. These were the enhanced versions of the schools run by kings in those times. For example, the first public school in the United States opened in the 17th century.

As the industrial revolution blew to full scale, it transformed the entire schooling system. Industries needed people with specific skills and there had to be someone to teach those skills. The development of science and technology added more things to be taught to the population. Access to information became widespread and people started to be educated about education, increasing the demand for a schooling system. This gave rise to the classroom schooling system we have even today.

Schools are no more limited to teach how to read and write, do some basic survival-level math, or instill faith or patriotism. Physics, chemistry, calculus, algebra, biology, medicine, art, science—the number of skills to be taught multiplied, all driven by the continued industrial revolution. There was no more one-size curriculum. But leaving this to local authorities didn't turn out to be great. There was a need for the authority to step in and standardize the schooling system to teach the kids "the skills of the future."

What did we do to transform the school system to meet the demands of the industrial revolution? We brought the principles from the industries and applied them to the educational system. We moved from a single-school system to a multischool system with various classrooms inside of separate schools. Students are classified into cohorts with tailored curricula meeting the set requirements for each level (or class). Instruction manuals have been developed to ensure quality standards (textbooks). Quality control mechanisms are put in place to make sure the products are maturing the way they are intended (exams). The best-grade products (students) are sent to first-grade consumers (companies) and the next-grade products are sent to the lower-grade consumers. This is the transformation industrial society, Society 3.0, brought along.

This system continued into Society 4.0 with some enhancements and is also the system we use today. However, the digital revolution Society 4.0 enabled easy access to information (knowledge) and catapulted learning into the cyberspace. This particularly proved to be fruitful when the COVID-19 pandemic hit as the classrooms and schools were closed but shifted to virtual spaces. Imagine the suffering all the kids in the world would have gone through if there was no access to online learning for all of them, as was probably the case back in 1918 to 1920 during the Spanish flu. This is the power information society brought along to the system of education.

We no longer need to sit in a classroom to learn. Internet can answer a question, tell us the world's time, take us to the dream destination, entertain us, teach us complicated concepts, and let us do virtually anything. In fact, we don't even have to visit the Internet. All you need to do is ask the virtual assistant on a laptop or a cellphone and she pretty much will come up with an answer, most of the times informative and sometimes funny. Ask Fire TV to show you a specific educational video and it will play it for you. In a nutshell, digital revolution transformed the learning process by improving access to knowledge significantly.

Wait a minute. Didn't we say not too long ago that the schooling system hasn't changed? Yes, that's correct. Although the learning methods have improved significantly, the core values of formal education are at least over a century old, due for an overhaul. The question is, with the advent of Society 5.0, how should our education work and change? A complete overhaul over a night like stock prices is impossible to achieve especially with deeply entrenched values and habits of people associated. It involves every entity—from governments and schools to teachers, parents, and students. Hence, instead of predicting how educational system will be, I will focus on how it should be. If you are an entrepreneur, perhaps your next EdTech can spark that change.

How Should Education Behave in Future?

If there's any question parents, schools, and curriculum experts alike have been asking, it's what domain of study is good for children and what is not. In general, technology, math, chemistry, biology, physics, and medicine are some of the supposedly important departments that students are drawn to. Which subjects are "good" for today's kids, which are bound to make our kids "successful," and what our schools should teach—today's stakeholders ask these questions more than ever. But with knowledge widespread on the Internet, the focus of formal schooling should be to help develop foundational skills that will help future diamonds to excel in any field. The focus shouldn't be on *what* to teach students, but rather *how* to do it so as it becomes a lifelong lesson.

On that note, these well-known 4Cs, including six more to what I call the 10Cs of education, should define the future of education irrespective of the domain:

Communication

The world revolves around communication. All the great leaders ever lived and successful people in the world have one thing in common: they are good communicators. Teaching kids effective communication skills never goes off the syllabus. Remember, communication is not just about speaking, but also about listening. To communicate well, you need to learn to articulate your ideas as well as develop active listening skills.

Collaboration

Humans are social beings. They can't work alone for long. Working together has been a human trait for thousands of years which in modern terms is called team work. Team work is a prerequisite to developing leadership skills. The schools of the 21st century should focus on teaching students to solve problems by both effective communication and collaboration.

Critical Thinking

A skill that comes handy in every walk of life, critical thinking is an essential backbone of problem solving. It's all about analyzing the data, pondering the odds, and arriving at decisions. Critical thinking is indeed a skill one can learn. There are methods that help identify and use the right data to come up to a feasible solution to a problem. All of us are critical thinkers; it's just that this skill requires more practice, and the brain gets wired to do this better over time.

Creativity

As a kid, I read a book by Shiv Khera that said "Winners don't do different things. They do things differently." Creativity could be the difference between winners and losers, which can also be developed through careful focus in schools. Art, writing, building, storytelling, and even gaming are a few examples of activities that help develop this important skill.

These 4Cs are the well-known foundational skills that apply to any field of study and specialization and are recognized by the U.S. Department of Education and some other governments around the world. However, while they lay the strongest foundation to grow in any career students choose, they are far from complete when it comes to holistic education. There are few more Cs which when added will strengthen the 4Cs, if not complete them.

Confidence

The best gift we can give to any student is the gift of confidence. Our educational system must keep this at the center of the process. Regardless of what a student is interested in, help her do that confidently and without the fear of being judged. If there is one "right" skill to teach, I would argue it is to teach kids the fine line between arrogance and confidence.

Choice

Conventional education must give way to modern education facilitated by technology. Students must be given the chance to excel in what they are interested in, thus making the earlier question "what domain of study is good for children" irrelevant. Parents shouldn't push kids to pursue anything in particular because a certain skill is in demand. Rather, they should let them pursue what makes their children happy. Anything that makes someone happy has a higher chance of succeeding at than something you dread doing throughout your lifetime, especially when the first 4Cs are mastered. This choice is important to build the previous "C"—confidence.

Control

Let the students control their career. Let's not allow some system defined to fit everyone determine the future of our students. An extension to the previous "C" choice, control takes it one step further. It's not just what students want to learn, but also when and how they want to learn it, at their own pace. For example, if a first-grade student wants to learn third-grade math, let him do so. However, control should not be confused with freedom.

Connectivity

In this connected world, students have access to a lot of information on the Internet and it's essential to get them connected to this information. This connectivity will also allow them choose and control what they want to learn. Students do not have to learn in a classroom setting any longer. They can learn from wherever and whenever, as long as they have access to the Internet. However, it's also essential to enable the right type of connectivity, only to the right type of content, away from the bad actors and the shady side of the Internet.

Coaching

Now, if I am asking students to learn off the Internet, what role will the teacher play? Here is how it might work. Students currently attend schools to listen to lectures and take some work home for practice, called homework, a word a lot of kids hate. Let's flip that. With digital access to lectures, they can be followed any time from home, often from the best professor. And the "homework" can be done in school with the help of teachers. Or even better, coaches. However, most importantly, coaches should be working toward cultivating most of the Cs we talked about: communication, collaboration, critical thinking, creativity, confidence, and so on. All teachers should turn into coaches with the primary aim to discover the inherent talent in kids so they can cultivate their own talent rather than learning something that never interested them. Most importantly, coaches should help students navigate the complex society and ongoing information overload.

Classroom

Where will the earlier said "coaching" take place? In the classrooms. The last "C" in my list is the classroom, which will continue to have a very key role to play in the futuristic education. Future classrooms should be the breeding grounds for the various Cs we referred to earlier instead of "teaching machines," guiding the 21st-century students toward a better and brighter future.

Besides, note that to facilitate a seamless learning environment, home, classroom, and the outside world must fuse with one another. This 360-degree learning is what I believe is the future of education.

If 10Cs are too many, let me try and further summarize the future of education in three alphabets: the 3Ws. That is, www. I'm not referring to the web here, although it is the key enabler to the next-generation learning. Instead, it refers to learn *whatever*, *whenever*, and *wherever* and with no people judging you in your performance. This is analogous to the future of work. Education and work after all go hand in hand.

While all this looks good in theory, it may come across as a radical change to some. The pragmatic part of implementation is like swallowing a dead dart frog. First, the change must be "gradual," not an abrupt one. Second, not only do we need to change systems, we need to change ourselves, too, at least in the way we think. Of course, technology will enable this.

CHAPTER 5

The Roadmap to the BIG Future

Technology is transforming every industry from their roots of fundamental operation to the leaves of their working culture. Technology is going to dominate our lives completely like we have never seen before. Almost everyone on planet Earth will be impacted by technology directly or indirectly. Most importantly, it has become much more relevant for entrepreneurs and service seekers alike, especially jobs involving the creation of capital. There is absolutely no doubt about it.

Until now, how to navigate the bright, yet complicated future had been scattered throughout the book. It's time all of those points are raked together and each of them scrutinized to pave a roadmap toward the *big* future.

The future of everything will have one thing in common—work reduction, one of the three Ws discussed earlier. Work reduction will take place in multiple ways, but certainly more automation will be a part of every industry. The question in everyone's mind is: does it mean our jobs will be taken away? Let me try and address the elephant in the room.

The answer to this question is yes. Most jobs as they stand today will disappear in the future. Pretty disappointing, isn't it? How can the future be *big* if jobs are eliminated?

The headlines of the following news articles from some of the reputed news outlets are the harbingers of what is to happen.

"Robot Automation Will 'Take 800 Million Jobs by 2030': Report" —BBC News (2017).

"Robots Could Take 20 Million Manufacturing Jobs by 2030" —CNN wrote (Tappe 2019).

"Pandemic Wave of Automation May Be Bad News for Workers" —*New York Times* headlined in July 2021 (Casselman 2021).

Admittedly, the picture I painted might be toward the grimmer side for you. However, the title of this book states the opposite. That's because there is good news within all of this.

The good news is what we reviewed thus far is just one side of the tech coin and sadly the side that gets most of the spotlight in the media and elsewhere. The other side of the tech coin is bright and extremely hopeful. You should know how to see the other side and that's exactly what I attempt to do.

Let's start this discussion with a few common misconceptions or myths related to technology.

Myths of Automation

Myth 1—Automation Is Here to Eat Your Lunch

The facts we often forget are that automation is the generic term used for a plethora of things that cover AI and robotics and that automation is man-made. It's not some evil force conjured up by demons or a set of tools aliens sent to destroy earth. Automation was purposed to help us, not to hurt. The reason we want our printer to automatically order cartridges before they run out is not to take away that pleasurable task of buying cartridge but rather to help us by ensuring consistent supply of ink. You can extrapolate this example to everything automation touches, domestic or commercial.

The robotic helper on the factory floor or inside of a dangerous mine is to help ensure your safety and improve your productivity. It has no intention or incentive to take away your job. The purpose of the virtual financial risk analysis bot or the construction designer bot is to improve your efficiency. AI isn't conscious enough to take your job away; though this idea sounds the dumbest, let's clear that up because when it comes to intention, AI is spotless.

Automation Has No Intention to Eat Our Lunch

Although automation is designed to help us, it is more effective than humans. After all, its purpose is to improve our efficiency. For example, a robotic arm on the factory floor operated by a robotic operator may do the job of five workers. This is effectively eliminating 80 percent of the jobs: four out of five. This is an unfortunate and undisputable side effect. The point I want to drive is: automation will reduce the work, not eliminate it. Every profession in the world will need people; we will need less to produce more results. So, our lunch is not completely eaten by automation: each portion of the lunch is getting smaller. This is the first important thing.

The Portions Are Only Getting Smaller

The million-dollar fact we often ignore is there will be more lunch boxes, many times more, than boxes gone, although each lunch box might have smaller portions. Instead of grabbing one lunch box, grab two, maybe three or more. Let's take the factory floor example again. While the robotic arm has consolidated five jobs into one, thanks to automation, we are now able to produce more. More production will lead to cheaper prices. Cheaper prices will make products more accessible to everyone. What does this all mean? The demand goes up and also the overall quantity we produce. While the five jobs are consolidated into one, the overall production might have gone up by many folds. The net result is that the total number of jobs could be the same, maybe slightly less, or in fact, they may even be more than "preautomation" levels.

Automation Equals More Demand; More Demand Never Equals Less Jobs

Most people do not factor in the increase in productivity and affordability the mere increase in demand through automation has brought. Now, add the overall population growth to this equation. Global population is growing at a rate of 1 percent each year (Roser, Ritchie, Ortiz-Ospina 2019). The United Nations Department of Economic and Social Affairs predicts that the population levels will reach almost 10 billion by 2050 (2019). The growth in population directly means there will be more demand. More demand means increase in production. To keep up with that level of production, the industrial setup that sources the raw materials also needs to be revamped. Moreover, the products these industries make create more service-oriented jobs that were not there. That equals newer types of jobs and hence more number of lunch boxes. It's just that the jobs at a specific level were axed to replace a job in a significantly different domain of expertise. The only bad news that'll follow is that while some workers should upgrade their skills to work in the automated setting, others must learn new skills to take on the new set of jobs created. However, the central principle of automation is about creating more jobs, not less.

The factory floor example is just one use case. There are several others where jobs are almost completely eliminated. Take truck drivers, for example. Long-distance trucking will become autonomous very soon. Sure, drivers may still be needed on local roads. However, a greater number of hours driven by robots (trucks) and less by humans shouldn't blow our minds in the future. Will increase in transportation needs in general offset all the autonomous hours logged by the trucks? Will all the truck drivers have enough number of hours to drive to earn the same level they make today, if not more? Add drones and robotic transport to the mix. While nothing can be exactly predicted, a simple back-of-the-napkin sketch tells me that *a significant* number out of the 3.5 million truck drivers in the United States will lose their jobs.

This applies to various other sectors, too. If grocery stores become autonomous, despite there being more stores to meet the increased demand, will that number offset the number of jobs taken away by automation? The contribution of online and omni-channel shopping certainly does paint a grim picture for the brick-and-mortar stores.

Technology constantly creates new types of lunches even though it takes away many. But it's merely the titles that go away. Automation transposes and transports the titles to places which will only become evident on the journey. In order to adapt to the change, you must consistently develop your taste and get used to eating new types of lunch. That is the only way to survive the future. If you can figure this out, you will not just survive, but you will beat the trend.

Enough Lunch for Everyone. Some Will Need to Develop New Eating Habits

Let's look at some of the recent trends. Recently, many taxi drivers lost their jobs to ride-sharing services. But millions became their own taxi drivers through the likes of Uber. Technology created new lunch boxes: the ones who developed a taste for it can eat. And think about what it did to lifestyle in general. How often do you still call a taxi? You need a ride, just Uber. How often do you even drive your own car? And how many people are making extra cash through part-time driving?

Let's take another example. It is evident that AI is replacing financial advisors. But who is building those AI-based advisors? Do you think some software developers are building those in a vacuum or are they built autonomously? The fintech revolution is not aimed at eliminating financial sector jobs, but rather converting them into the fintech world from traditional financial world. All the fintech applications need financial analysts—the same analysts who would have given you financial advice manually. And when getting an advice from an AI is so laid-back and inexpensive compared to the pricy hourly rate a human charges, more people will get the advice, increasing the demand for financial services. More demand means more jobs for financial analysts. This is simply converting the type of lunch folks in the financial services industry must get used to.

More examples and I will rest my case. Travel-tech companies such as Orbitz disrupted the traditional travel agents. Airbnb disrupted the hospitality industry. Home cooking apps disordered the restaurant businesses. Private rental car companies such as Turo unsettled the traditional rental car businesses. But they created income opportunities for an entirely different set of people along the way. There are good examples of jobs getting shifted from one subsector to another within the same industry. But what about jobs eliminated in one industry altogether, but added in an entirely new industry? It's kind of a lunch, but in a completely different cuisine. For example, the space industry is new and booming. Do you know how many people it employs as of today? Around 183,000 in the United States alone (Space Foundation Editorial Team 2020). This number is expected to grow exponentially. Biotech is creating so many jobs every day. Renewable energy jobs are skyrocketing. AI developers are always in demand. I will give you some futuristic skills to focus on shortly, but the point is very clear. You must constantly upgrade your skills and be prepared to survive off a new type of lunch, because change is the only constant that'll sustain forever.

Myth 2—Only Low-Level Jobs Are at Risk of Disappearing Through Automation

By now, we've discussed that technology will only move jobs around, either within the same industry or across industries, and it may end up creating more jobs than that exist today. But who will have to bear the brunt of a change of such a massive scale? Whether it's a gentle touch or a vehement push, everyone's going to be affected. The best thing to do is to move in the direction of its force, so you take advantage of it instead of resisting. That entails upskilling and cross-skilling oneself in more than one subdomain toward the direction of technology flow.

However, we can use certain principles to understand the impact of the "tech-touch." It is a common misconception that only blue-collar jobs will be impacted by technology and automation. Whatever people's definition of collar-jobs is, technology treats all types of jobs equally. Take surgeons, for example. Surgery is considered one of the high-level jobs in terms of expertise, prestige, and pay. But robots perform surgeries with higher precision than human surgeons. With all due respect, they won't leave scissors inside our body. They will not operate on your left leg instead of the right, by mistake. They do not have to worry about being awake all night and making some minor, but expensive error. They can incise the site with precision. And most important of all, they can perform surgeries all day and night and won't complain about it. However, it is not to say that they will replace all human surgeons.

Myth 3—Software Developers Are Immune to Automation and Technology

Let's take another example of software developers. With all the hype about technology and IT being such an integral part of future technology, how can the future sustain without software developers? Well, remember AI writes its own code. That's the fundamental premise of AI. If AI is writing its code, why do we need software developers? Moreover, with the rise in so many low-code and no-code tools, software development is really becoming old fashion. Keep in mind though that I am referring to software development only, not information technology as a whole. Although many combine these two terms, they are not one and the same. AI developers, for example, will have a bright future. Though AI might be better at innovation and replication, it doesn't exceed humans in rational and cross-disciplinary thinking.

Beating Innovation in Its Game

To understand which jobs are impacted to what extent, it's best to understand what machines are good at and what they are not. We know that machines can think fast and they can do laborious tasks, meaning machines have better brains than us (in general). And when it comes to muscle power, humans are no match to machines. What are machines not good at then? Here are a few.

Hand–eye coordination: It's very difficult to build a machine with good hand–eye coordination. While advances are underway, it's easier to hire humans where hand–eye coordination is important. Service technicians, mechanics, hygienists, dentists, fire fighters, military personnel, and even surgeons are good examples. This is a stark reminder that not all jobs are equal.

Emotional element: Machines can do a lot of tasks better than us, but one thing they lack is emotion, at least for now. Has someone called you a machine because you failed to show emotions? I have been called a machine a few times for this reason. But isn't that the beauty of a machine? A lot of jobs rely on these emotions. Doctors, nurses, adult care workers, social workers, and teachers are just a subset. In fact, this human touch is required in almost all jobs. Again, that part will stay with humans across all industries and the rest may be outsourced to machines.

Creative thinking: While machines can do a great job in computing large sums of data, they are not creative thinkers. Advanced AI is trying to change this, but it is still going to be based upon certain algorithms. General-purpose AI is supposed to be creative, but creativity is not something that can easily be taught to the machines. Your creative mind will not be taken over by a machine, not any time soon. If you are an artist, an author, a designer, or a public relationship manager, chances are that machines will still try to copy you but barely to that level. Well, technology might assist you, no doubt, but your creative mind will keep you going. However, it is not to say that only few jobs require creative thinking. The future will push humans in the creative part of every job and use machines for the more autonomous functions.

Consciousness and ethics: Machines do not realize that they are machines, though they can be trained to say that. Machines can *say*, but they can't *be*. On that note, artificial consciousness as a concept is under development, but it's a long way to go before something concrete comes out of it. Let me give you a scenario. You are driving at 50 miles per hour. Suddenly, a kid flashes on one side of the road and an old woman, on the opposite. You can only save one of them, not both. What will the AI pick? Yeah—the common ethical dilemma, right?

Humans use their consciousness-driven selective ethics and make some on-the-spot decisions, despite the consequences. However, this is a popular ethical question, which still remains to be answered. Until those are all sorted out, humans are still required to make such decisions. Call it a human overwrite, if you will. Every field will need human intervention. Machines are not yet ready to run the show on their entirety. The key here is to use machines for what they are good at. Humans will do the rest. A teamwork!

In a nutshell, not all jobs will be replaced by technology. Every field will need humans. We are not ready for a fully autonomous society yet. Jobs will be consolidated. Some jobs will be moved to a different area within the same industry and some to an entirely different industry.

The History of Automation-Infused Anxiety

This discussion today is tied to the fourth industrial revolution, the one we are entering now. There is a lot of speculation in the media around upcoming job losses to automation. Why is this called the fourth industrial revolution? Simply because there have been three prominent industrial transformations thus far already. The world didn't lose all the jobs during those reforms. On the contrary, we created jobs, global economy skyrocketed, and our general standard of living improved tremendously. Let's look at each one of them with the lens of job loss or, rather, I should say job creation.

First Industrial Revolution

The first industrial revolution marks the beginning of the third-generation society (Society 3.0) that moved from agricultural society into an industrial one in the 18th and 19th centuries. It was mainly centered on steam power, predominantly fueled by coal. Economies transformed from high (and for the most part, only) dependency on farming to more of urban and industry settings. The first job that got impacted by this revolution was farming. Development of tools made farming easier. The end results? The number of farming jobs was cut. Vast stretches of agricultural land were converted into industrial sites, resulting in less farming land, which in turn resulted in less farming jobs.

The advent of modern tools and technologies resulted in the loss of farming jobs. But does that mean there are no farmers today? In fact, jobs are never lost, only skills are redundant. Farmers who would use muscle power to plough fields lost their jobs to people who use tillers to do the same task.

In the same manner, in the transition from agro-society to an industrial one, physical farming skills were swapped with technical machine skills. It created so many factory jobs and gave rise to multiple new jobs—rail roads, new type of construction, development of various machineries, and use of machines. We used to have only two classes of societal status before: the rich and the poor. The industrial revolution created a new societal status: the middle class. Can you imagine our life today without the industrial revolution? No human would have moved beyond physical forces, let alone build sophisticated computers. Farming and trading would be our only professions. However, finding a job would be equally difficult then, too.

But the first industrial revolution was not a smooth sailing. It created a lot of anxiety among people and rightfully so. Yes, it did create a temporary job loss, similar to how the fourth industrial revolution will result in a job disruption. And in many cases, it would result in a chaotic situation, resulting in higher numbers of unemployment-related problems. The BBC News wrote on April 20, 2012:

> They burned down mills in the name of a mythical character called Ludd. In the midst of the British industrial revolution, skilled textile workers feared for their jobs. An uprising began in 1811 when Nottinghamshire weavers attacked the new automated looms that were replacing them. The machine breaking spread to West Yorkshire wool workers and Lancashire cotton mills, in what the historian Eric Hobsbawm called "collective

bargaining by riot. Machinery was wrecked, mills were burned down and the Luddites fought pitched battles with the British Army." (Castella 2012)

Your postthought argument here. For example, transformation is always neutral. While textile machines were good for mass production, they took the jobs away from the hard-earning hand-knitters. While violence cannot be justified, the degree of "exponentiality" of a technology determines the "shock value" of that generation. If the shock value is higher, the repercussions of that transformation might also be unexpected.

Second Industrial Revolution

Generally described as the era of electricity, the second industrial revolution predominantly transformed the steam into electric power bringing further efficiencies to the process. Petroleum became a more prominent source of energy leading to the invention of combustible engine. But this also meant that steam-powered engines were converted to electricity. The skills acquired over time to operate all that machinery was now gone and a lot of folks had to be reskilled. But it was not just a matter of upskilling. It eliminated a lot of jobs. For example, the invention of the light bulb eliminated the jobs of lamplighters and "gas-lighters" responsible for lighting our cities at night. You can call this particular phenomenon "the automation of street lights." There were reports of gas-lighter strikes resisting this revolution.

But imagine what the second industrial revolution brought along. Automobiles, airplanes, mass production, buildings as they exist today—none of those would have been possible. Millions of jobs never ever imagined were created, jobs such as managers and machine operators. Did second industrial revolution take away jobs or added to the total? I will let you answer that question. But did it stop the "Luddites" from complaining? No.

When I was a kid, an old neighbor came home miserable from work. He feared he would lose his job to a robot (traffic light) the local government was going to install. He was a policeman in the traffic department, and his job was to control traffic, standing under the hot sun the entire day directing traffic at intersections. Needless to say, the traffic light never took away his job. He was moved to a different area which was less challenging than spending the whole day under the hot sun, breathing in the exhaust fumes from the vehicles and hearing the whirring and humming noises from them until he retired with a complete set of benefits. While it didn't eliminate his "job" per se, his skill became redundant.

Third Industrial Revolution

The third industrial revolution, also known as the digital revolution, happened in the second half of the 20th century and transformed our society from analog to digital.

The third industrial revolution both added and took away a lot of jobs. For example, "computer" used to be a job before computers became widespread. People would get employed as computers, making a living doing what today's computers are designed to do, however, with less accuracy and diligence. Those human computers lost their jobs to actual computers. But was that a total conversion? Of course not. They were simply moved to different areas to do different types of jobs, either using the same skills or through upskilling.

The digital revolution-led fear of job loss can still be felt in our homes. My dad used to work as a clerk in a shipping company. When his company bought computers, they all feared that their jobs would be taken away in a flash. But they never did. Sure, they had to learn to use computers. Instead of using a typewriter, calculator, and a lot of manual calculations, my dad performed those operations on a computer. Computers ended up making their jobs easier, sending my dad home happy at the end of each day. He worked in the same company until he retired.

Digital revolution without doubt eliminated a lot of jobs. However, many more were created in the course of this transformation inciting thousands of people to upskill their talent. Computer analysts, data entry specialists, software analysts, software developers, web designers, and cyber security analysts were the professional names of many people who later gained expertise in "using computers." Information technology employs an estimated three million people in the United States alone. In the grand scheme of things, did the third industrial revolution eliminate jobs in total or was the net result the addition of jobs? That surely is a rhetorical question.

Fears are associated with the fourth industrial revolution the same way they did before. Will this new revolution eat our lunch or will it actually create more lunch? If history tells us anything, the upcoming chapter in our lives will undoubtedly be a mixed one for all of us. However, there's a catch. The future will not be *big* all by itself. We need to make it big. Technology has all the potential to crush us if we do not know how to take advantage of it. The key is to understand what the future has to offer and then gain the skills required, not just to survive in the next-generation society but to benefit from it.

Future of Work

The change in technological sophistication changes the pattern of employment. Gone are the days when you depended on full-time employment and when you had to work in a 9-to-5 office six days a week.

Before we discuss the future, let's take a trip back in history as we did thus far with everything else. Generations of farmers; generations of goldsmiths; generations of fishermen: people were predominantly "born" into a type of work as the "trades" were getting passed on to generations for the longest time. The concept of a "job" was rare, and the concept of job security was even rarer.

Industrialization in Society 3.0 transformed the work scene by bringing about jobs in factories as well as the offices tied to those factories, giving rise to 9-to-5 jobs. While many of these factory jobs were not known to provide a long-term safety net in the beginning, that changed over time, driven by factors such as unionization and government interference. My dad's generation stayed in their jobs for life. Like him, most people started and ended their careers in the same place.

This was the second industrial revolution days. In the digital revolution era, which is right now, how many people stay in a job for half a decade, let alone a lifetime? How many of them work a single job for a single employer? The median number of years someone works for their employer stays at 4.1 years in January 2020, infinitesimally bigger than the 2018 data—4.2 years, according to a news release from the Bureau of Labor Statistics (2020).

Society 4.0 changed "job for a lifetime" trend to switching jobs every five years or so on an average. How is the future work going to look like? Will the work-span shrink further? Expand again? Let's delve in.

I believe it will be driven by another set of 3Ws—Whatever, Wherever, and Whenever. It's all about freedom to do what you want to do, when you want to do, and where you want to do from.

Work Whatever

Forget about getting a "job" if you don't like full-time employment. Be an entrepreneur, doing whatever you like. Digital revolution started this trend and it is not only going to continue but will grow. Turning an idea into reality is so easy and inexpensive these days that anyone with a good working idea can become an entrepreneur. Starting a company required renting an office space, buying expensive equipment, and potentially hiring staff in the past. In the digital era, all you need to launch your company is a laptop. Well, depending upon what you want to do, even a laptop may not be needed. You can get some space on the cloud, develop your product digitally, and market it in the virtual space through social media. The investment needed could be as close to zero dollars as possible, just laying out your skills. This will only continue to become easier, as the opportunities grow exponentially in the future across all three B.I.G. technologies.

However, it doesn't mean you *have* to become an entrepreneur. You can put your multiple skills into action through the gig economy, too.

Work Whenever

Employees no longer have to work a single job. In fact, employees no longer have to remain as employees. Switching jobs every five years or so is already becoming an old trend. The postpandemic, postrealization ethos of work is: become your own boss and work whenever you feel like it. Well, you could technically do that if you are an entrepreneur.

But thanks to gig economy, you can do that without having to start anything on your own. You technically partner with a company on a temporary basis. For example, you can partner with Uber to be their driver. You work whenever you have time. You have something to take care of? Just clock out and take care of what you need to. There is no boss looking over your shoulder and no one controlling your hours. Taxi drivers through the likes of Uber and Lyft; food delivery workers, such as Uber Eats and Doordash; and tour guides and hosts, such as Airbnb, are a few examples. Companies such as Upwork and Fiverr that offer platforms to freelancers have become the new employment norm. Upwork has been named in *The Times*'s list of "100 Most Influential Companies" of 2022. In this modern marketplace, you don't necessarily have to stick to one job. You can put your multiple skills into action. You can take up that logo design work in the morning when you are home, be a tour guide in the afternoon, and an Uber driver in the evening. You would be surprised to know that 36 percent of the U.S. workforce hustle in the gig economy (as of March 2022), bringing this number to an estimated 57.3 million (Duszyński 2022). And this is only expected to grow.

Work Wherever

It's not just the 9-to-5 jobs that are transforming; the whole concept of office culture is changing. Most jobs of the future can be executed from anywhere. For example, do you remember the future miners that mine from a computer in the metaverse? Not the crypto mining, but actual mineral mining. If you work from behind a computer, how does it matter where you are located? You can work from home. And that home can be on a beach. Or you can move from one place to another, visiting all the exotic places around the globe while still working because all you will need for your future job is a computer. Whether meeting with a client or collaborating, there are numerous tools that have been decreasing the convenience margin of in-person and virtual meeting every day. Video conferencing will move to the metaverse in the future, making it an immersive experience through immersion technologies and making you feel like you are really in the same location together with others in the meeting. And this trend was further fueled and accelerated by COVID-19. Many companies, predominantly in the IT world, are announcing that work-from-anywhere is here to stay.

Think about the impact this trend will create. The first result of this trend will impact the population density. There will not be a need to live around city centers and other "official hubs" any longer. Population will be spread to suburban and even rural locations from city centers. The trend has already begun in countries like the United States.

Closing

There is a common myth that you must be a geek to survive in the tech world. That is absolutely not true. No one really knows technology to its full extent. For example, if you think a software developer is a geek, think again. A software developer has no idea of the 0s and 1s that goes inside the computer. There are many abstract layers built on top to make the job of a software developer easy. The developers simply need to learn a programming language, which does all the job in the background. A rocket scientist may not entirely understand the science behind the rocket. A biotech engineer may not know how gene editing exactly occurs in the backend. Learn technology to the extent you can. While it is true that the more you learn novelties, the merrier it is, any amount of tech knowledge will help you to the point that it almost becomes mandatory in the future.

However, there's always a tiny corner spot for those who think technology is not to their taste. There are a lot of areas within the tech world that require least technology knowledge or skill. Take data scientist, for example. That's a hot skill of the future, but you could be a data scientist with less and less technical skills. You only need to understand the data well. However, with only an understanding of that sort, the data skills might slowly be taken over by another advanced analysis tool and that's how exactly skills become redundant. It will help to have a minimal understanding of how data can be used by the technology you are delivering these data to, in order to extend the skill's expiry date. Going deeper into technology will only help secure your future. And for those who think technology is not their cup of tea, think again. Because if you don't, you'll have to think it over for the rest of your life.

All good things must come to an end. This beautiful, B.I.G. journey is also approaching toward one. I want to remind you that the future has a lot to offer. But it's also going to be complicated, and it will be *big* for you only if you know how to navigate it. Do not let anyone make you believe that the technology is here to get you. Be smart about it. Learn how to exploit it, because opportunities are endless. There are two things that never stop in life: learning and selling. Keep learning new trends and sell yourself out there, no matter what career you pursue.

References

Chapter 1

Dorey, F. August 2, 2021. "How Have We Changed since Our Species First Appeared?" *The Australian Museum.* https://australian.museum/learn/science/human-evolution/how-have-we-changed-since-our-species-first-appeared/.

Encyclopedia of Communication and Information. August 2, 2022. "Information Society, Description of." www.encyclopedia.com/media/encyclopedias-almanacs-transcripts-and-maps/information-society-description.

Greshko, M. May 3, 2021. "These Early Humans Lived 300,000 Years Ago-But Had Modern Faces." National Geographic. www.nationalgeographic.com/history/article/morocco-early-human-fossils-anthropology-science.

National Geographic Society. July 8, 2022 "The Development of Agriculture." https://education.nationalgeographic.org/resource/development-agriculture.

Chapter 3

Amitay, E.L., A. Gies, K. Weigl, and H. Brenner. 2019. "Fecal Immunochemical Tests for Colorectal Cancer Screening: Is Fecal Sampling from Multiple Sites Necessary?" *Cancers* 11, no. 3, p. 400. https://doi.org/10.3390/cancers11030400.

Blanco, S. August 10, 2022. "Electric Cars' Turning Point May Be Happening as U.S. Sales Numbers Start Climb." *Car and Driver.* www.caranddriver.com/news/a39998609/electric-car-sales-usa/.

Brown, J.E. 2022. "Team Builds the First Living Robots." *University of Vermont.* www.uvm.edu/news/story/team-builds-first-living-robots (accessed August 15, 2022).

Cheng, R. May 18, 2018. "A 150-Mph Underground Commute—That's How Elon Musk Plans to Solve LA's Traffic Problem." CNET. www.cnet.com/culture/elon-musks-boring-company-wants-to-charge-1-for-a-150-mph-loop-ride-space-x-tesla/.

Dilanian, K. December 3, 2020. "China Has Done Human Testing to Create Biologically Enhanced Super Soldiers, Says Top U.S. Official." *NBCNews.* NBCUniversal News Group. www.nbcnews.com/politics/national-security/china-has-done-human-testing-create-biologically-enhanced-super-soldiers-n1249914.

Ewing, J. August 5, 2021. "President Biden Sets a Goal of 50 Percent Electric Vehicle Sales by 2030." *New York Times*. www.nytimes.com/2021/08/05/business/biden-electric-vehicles.html.

Furmage, G. April 6, 2018. "Watch: Mind-Reading Headset Can Understand the Voice in Your Head." *Sunday Post*. www.sundaypost.com/fp/watch-mind-reading-headset-can-understand-the-voice-in-your-head/.

Fox, M. October 13, 2016. "Brain Chip Helps Paralyzed Man Feel His Fingers." *NBCNews.com*. www.nbcnews.com/health/health-news/brain-chip-helps-paralyzed-man-feel-his-fingers-n665881.

Gohd, C. April 9, 2021. "NASA to Land 1st Person of Color on the Moon with Artemis Program." *Space*. www.space.com/nasa-sending-first-person-of-color-to-moon-artemis.

Gugliotta, G. July 1, 2008. "The Great Human Migration." Smithsonian.com. Smithsonian Institution. www.smithsonianmag.com/history/the-great-human-migration-13561/.

Holley, I.B. 1997. "Technology and Doctrine." In *Technology and the Air Force: A Retrospective Assessment*. Washington, DC: United States Air Force.

Huang, M.Yan. July 22, 2021. "Elon Musk's Hyperloop Concept Could Become the Fastest Way to Travel." *Business Insider*. www.businessinsider.com/how-the-hyperloop-could-be-the-fastest-way-to-travel-2020-12.

Johnson, E.M. July 20, 2021. "'Road to Space': Billionaire Bezos Has Successful Suborbital Jaunt." *Reuters*. Thomson Reuters. www.reuters.com/technology/jeff-bezos-worlds-richest-man-set-inaugural-space-voyage-2021-07-20/.

Jones, B. September 29, 2017. "Elon Musk Plans to Make City-to-City Rocket Travel a Reality." *Futurism*. https://futurism.com/elon-musk-plans-to-make-city-to-city-rocket-travel-a-reality.

Kharpal, A. March 30, 2020. "Use of Surveillance to Fight Coronavirus Raises Concerns about Government Power after Pandemic Ends." *CNBC*. www.cnbc.com/2020/03/27/coronavirus-surveillance-used-by-governments-to-fight-pandemic-privacy-concerns.html.

Lambert, F. June 17, 2021. "Tesla Model S Plaid Breaks All the Records in First Independent Test, But 0-60 Mph Has a Caveat." *Electrek*. https://electrek.co/2021/06/17/tesla-model-s-plaid-breaks-records-in-first-independent-test-but-0-60-mph-caveat/.

Lederman, J. August 5, 2021. "Biden Signs Order Aiming for Half of New Vehicles to Be Electric by 2030." NBCNews.com. NBCUniversal News Group. www.nbcnews.com/politics/politics-news/biden-sign-order-aiming-half-new-vehicles-be-electric-2030-n1275995.

Mann, A., T. Pultarova, and E. Howell. April 14, 2022. "SpaceX Starlink Internet: Costs, Collision Risks and How It Works." *Space*. www.space.com/spacex-starlink-satellites.html.

Market Research Firm. n.d. "Smart Clothing Market." www.marketsandmarkets .com/Market-Reports/smart-clothing-market-56415040.html (accessed August 14, 2022).

Mozur, P. July 8, 2018. "Inside China's Dystopian Dreams: A.I., Shame and Lots of Cameras." *New York Times*. www.nytimes.com/2018/07/08/business/ china-surveillance-technology.html.

NASA. n.d. "Artemis." www.nasa.gov/specials/artemis/ (accessed August 15, 2022).

Neate, R. January 20, 2022. "Elon Musk's Brain Chip Firm Neuralink Lines up Clinical Trials in Humans." *Guardian*. Guardian News and Media. www .theguardian.com/technology/2022/jan/20/elon-musk-brain-chip-firm-neuralink-lines-up-clinical-trials-in-humans.

Park, K. April 28, 2022. "The Boring Company to Take on Hyperloop Project." TechCrunch. https://techcrunch.com/2022/04/24/elon-musks-the-boring-company-to-take-on-hyperloop-project/.

Projects. June 20, 2023. "The Boring Company." www.boringcompany.com/projects.

Rolt, C. and J. Allen. 1997. "Essay." In *The Steam Engine of Thomas Newcomen*, pp. 10–14. Ashbourne: Landmark.

Scrapehero. n.d. "Number of Amazon Go Locations in the United States in 2022." www.scrapehero.com/location-reports/Amazon%20Go-USA/ (accessed August 15, 2022).

Scutti, S. November 15, 2017. "FDA Oks Pill With Digital Tracking Device." *CNN*. Cable News Network. https://edition.cnn.com/2017/11/14/health/ fda-digital-pill-abilify/index.html.

Shih, J.J., D.J. Krusienski, and J.R. Wolpaw. 2012. "Brain-Computer Interfaces in Medicine." *Mayo Clinic proceedings* 87, no. 3, pp. 268–279. https://doi .org/10.1016/j.mayocp.2011.12.008.

Smith, M. April 5, 2022. "Amazon Orders Record Number of Launches for Kuiper Satellite Constellation." *Spacepolicyonline*. https://spacepolicyonline .com/news/amazon-orders-record-number-of-launches-for-kuiper-satellite-constellation/.

Suarez, A. March 29, 2022. "I Tested the Mirror to See If It Was Worth the Hype." *SFGATE*. www.sfgate.com/shopping/article/lululemon-Mirror-review-16924600.php.

Subbaraman, N. February 28, 2013. "Two Rats, Thousands of Miles Apart, Cooperate Telepathically Via Brain Implant." NBCNews. NBCUniversal News Group. www.nbcnews.com/sciencemain/two-rats-thousands-miles-apart-cooperate-telepathically-brain-implant-1c8608274.

The Boring Company. April 20, 2022. "Series C Round." www.boringcompany. com/seriescround.

The Wright Story/Inventing the Airplane/1901 Wright Glider Experiments. n.d. "Not Within A Thousand Years." www.wright-brothers.org/History_Wing/

Wright_Story/Inventing_the_Airplane/Not_Within_A_Thousand_Years/ Not_Within_A_Thousand_Years.htm (accessed August 6, 2022).

Toyota IE. August 10, 2022. "Toyota Has Lots of New Innovations Coming down the Line." www.toyota.ie/company/news/2021/solid-state-batteries.

Wall, M. August 11, 2022. "SpaceX's Starship Won't Launch on 1st Orbital Test Flight This Month." *Space*. www.space.com/spacex-starship-orbital-test-flight-launch-window.

World Health Organization. July 12, 2019. "Cancer." www.who.int/health-topics/cancer#tab=tab_1.

Yarow, J. January 2, 2014. "[Corrected] The Reason People Thought the Telephone Would Be a Total Flop." *Business Insider*. https://slate.com/business/2014/01/why-people-thought-telephones-would-fail.html.

Chapter 4

"National Restaurant Association Releases 2022 State of the Restaurant Industry Report." February 1, 2022. *National Restaurant Association Releases 2022 State of the Restaurant Industry Report*. National Restaurant Association. https://restaurant.org/research-and-media/media/press-releases/association-releases-2022-state-of-the-restaurant-industry-report/.

Amazon. August 9, 2022. "Amazon.com: Amazon Sidewalk: Amazon Devices & Accessories." www.amazon.com/Amazon-Sidewalk/b?node=21328123011.

Baggaley, K. December 21, 2017. "Robots Are Replacing Humans in the World's Mines. Here's Why." *NBCNews.com*. www.nbcnews.com/mach/science/robots-are-replacing-humans-world-s-mines-here-s-why-ncna831631.

Boffey, D. April 30, 2021. "Dutch Couple Become Europe's First Inhabitants of a 3D-Printed House." *Guardian*. Guardian News and Media. www.theguardian.com/technology/2021/apr/30/dutch-couple-move-into-europe-first-fully-3d-printed-house-eindhoven.

Burgherr, P. and S. Hirschberg. March 2005. "Accident Risks in the Energy Sector: Comparative Evaluations." U.S. Department of Energy. www.osti.gov/etdeweb/servlets/purl/20669892.

Buzby, J.C., H.F. Wells, and J. Hyman. February 2014. "The Estimated Amount, Value, and Calories of Postharvest Food Losses at the Retail and Consumer Levels in the United States." EIB-121, U.S. Department of Agriculture, Economic Research Service.

Castenson, J. April 5, 2021. "3D-Printed California Community Shows the Technology's Huge Potential for Home Construction." *Forbes*. Forbes Magazine. www.forbes.com/sites/jennifercastenson/2021/04/05/3d-printed-project-with-15-net-zero-energy-homes-is-just-the-tip-of-this-techs-future/?sh=17e6ca6f3f8c.

CFI Team. January 23, 2022. "Bretton Woods Agreement." Corporate Finance Institute. https://corporatefinanceinstitute.com/resources/knowledge/finance/bretton-woods-agreement/.

Chow, D. July 10, 2019. "Mission to Rare Metal Asteroid Could Spark Space Mining Boom." NBCNews. NBCUniversal News Group. www.nbcnews.com/mach/science/mission-rare-metal-asteroid-could-spark-space-mining-boom-ncna1027971.

Clement, J. n.d. "Topic: Online Gaming." *Statista*. www.statista.com/topics/1551/online-gaming/#dossierKeyfigures (accessed August 15, 2022).

Delbert, C. November 2, 2021. "The Dawn of Wireless Electricity Is Finally upon Us and New Zealand Is Giving It a Try." *Popular Mechanics*. https://www.popularmechanics.com/science/a33522699/wireless-electricity-new-zealand/.

Field Level Media. May 12, 2020. "Report: Gaming Revenue to Top $159B in 2020." *Reuters*. Thomson Reuters. www.reuters.com/article/esports-business-gaming-revenues-idUSFLM8jkJMl.

Ghizoni, S.K. November 22, 2013. "Nixon Ends Convertibility of U.S. Dollars to Gold and Announces Wage/Price Controls." *Federal Reserve History*. www.federalreservehistory.org/essays/gold-convertibility-ends.

Glacier Media Group. December 1, 2020. "Cobalt Demand From Battery Industry Expected to Grow in the Next Five Years—Report." www.mining.com/cobalt-demand-from-battery-industry-expected-to-grow-in-the-next-five-years-report/.

Glacier Media Group. June 28, 2021. "Green Copper Demand to Average 13% Annual Growth Over Next 10 Years—Report." www.mining.com/green-copper-demand-to-average-13-annual-growth-over-next-10-years-report/.

Glacier Media Group. September 3, 2019. "Global Wind Turbine Fleet to Consume over 5.5mt of Copper by 2028—Report." www.mining.com/global-wind-turbine-fleet-to-consume-over-5-5mt-of-copper-by-2028-report/.

Grand view research. March 11, 2019. "Smart Fabrics Market Size, Share & Trends Analysis Report By Product (Active, Very Smart), By End Use (Defense & Military, Sports & Fitness), By Functionality (Sensing, Energy Harvesting), And Segment Forecasts, 2019—2025." *Smart Fabrics Market Size, Share | Industry Analysis Report, 2019-2025*. www.grandviewresearch.com/industry-analysis/smart-textiles-industry.

Hayes, A. February 16, 2022. "History of the Dutch Tulip Bulb Market's Bubble." Investopedia. www.investopedia.com/terms/d/dutch_tulip_bulb_market_bubble.asp.

Johnson, M., ed. December 2, 2020. "Microbes to Demonstrate Biomining of Asteroid Material Aboard ISS." NASA. www.nasa.gov/mission_pages/station/research/news/bioasteroid-spacex-21.

Kann, D. August 12, 2020. "Regular Bricks Can Be Transformed into Energy Storage Devices." *CNN*. https://edition.cnn.com/2020/08/12/world/smart-bricks-energy-storage-solution-scn/index.html.

Macrotrends. August 12, 2022. "Amazon Net Worth 2010-2022: AMZN." www.macrotrends.net/stocks/charts/AMZN/amazon/net-worth.

Mitha, F. June 25, 2022. "Biomining: Turning Waste into Gold with Microbes." *Labiotech UG*. www.labiotech.eu/in-depth/biomining-sustainable-microbes/.

Mufson, S. January 29, 2021. "General Motors to Eliminate Gasoline and Diesel Light-Duty Cars and Suvs by 2035." *Washington Post*. WP Company. www.washingtonpost.com/climate-environment/2021/01/28/general-motors-electric/.

Musk, E (@elonmusk). February 26, 2021, 3.32 AM. Twitter Post. https://twitter.com/elonmusk/status/1365055830085763081?lang=en.

PETA. July 10, 2022. "Leather: Animals Abused and Killed for Their Skins." www.peta.org/issues/animals-used-for-clothing/animals-used-clothing-factsheets/leather-animals-abused-killed-skins/.

Placek, M. July 23, 2021. "Projected Global Battery Demand by Application." *Statista*. www.statista.com/statistics/1103218/global-battery-demand-forecast/.

Pramuk, J. November 16, 2021. "Biden Signs $1 Trillion Bipartisan Infrastructure Bill Into Law, Unlocking Funds for Transportation, Broadband, Utilities." *CNBC*. www.cnbc.com/2021/11/15/biden-signing-1-trillion-bipartisan-infrastructure-bill-into-law.html.

Rhodes, C.J. March 2010. "Solar Energy: Principles and Possibilities." *Science Progress*, pp. 37–112. https://doi.org/10.3184/003685010X12626410325807.

Showley, R. September 9, 2011. "Blackout's Economic Impact Mixed, Experts Say." *San Diego Union-Tribune*.

Smith, E. May 6, 2021. "Copper Is 'the New Oil' and Low Inventories Could Push It to $20,000 per Ton, Analysts Say." *CNBC*. www.cnbc.com/2021/05/06/copper-is-the-new-oil-and-could-hit-20000-per-ton-analysts-say.html.

SpaceX, May 21, 2020. "SmallsatRideshare Program." www.spacex.com/rideshare/.

Stevens, P. December 30, 2019. "The Battery Decade: How Energy Storage Could Revolutionize Industries in the Next 10 Years." *CNBC*. www.cnbc.com/2019/12/30/battery-developments-in-the-last-decade-created-a-seismic-shift-that-will-play-out-in-the-next-10-years.html.

Thomas, L. April 20, 2021. "Lululemon Is Testing a Resale Program Where Shoppers Can Sell and Buy Used Items." *CNBC*. www.cnbc.com/2021/04/20/lululemon-to-launch-resale-pilot-for-shoppers-to-sell-buy-used-items.html.

Toliver, Z. August 22, 2018. "Is Silk Vegan? for Every Pound, 3,000 Animals Are Killed." PETA. www.peta.org/blog/is-silk-vegan/.

Treadgold, T. August 12, 2019. "Gold Is Hot but Nickel Is Hotter as Demand Grows for Batteries in Electric Vehicles." *Forbes*. Forbes Magazine. www

.forbes.com/sites/timtreadgold/2019/08/11/gold-is-hot-but-nickel-is-hotter-as-demand-grows-for-batteries-in-electric-vehicles/?sh=1cb5d7cf3610.

U.S. Energy Information Administration (EIA). May 13, 2022. "Frequently Asked Questions (Faqs)—U.S. Energy Information Administration (EIA)." www.eia.gov/tools/faqs/faq.php?id=92&t=4.

US Census Bureau. 2016. "Historical Estimates of World Population." December 16, 2021. www.census.gov/data/tables/time-series/demo/international-programs/historical-est-worldpop.html.

Voutsinos, M. May 23, 2022. "Biomining the Elements of the Future." *Conversation*. https://theconversation.com/biomining-the-elements-of-the-future-87621.

Walsh, N.P. February 24, 2021. "CNN Exclusive: A Solar Panel in Space Is Collecting Energy That Could One Day Be Beamed to Anywhere on Earth." *CNN*. https://edition.cnn.com/2021/02/23/americas/space-solar-energy-pentagon-science-scn-intl/index.html.

Chapter 5

BBC. November 29, 2017. "Robot Automation Will 'Take 800 Million Jobs by 2030'—Report." www.bbc.com/news/world-us-canada-42170100.

Casselman, B. July 3, 2021. "Pandemic Wave of Automation May Be Bad News for Workers." *New York Times*. www.nytimes.com/2021/07/03/business/economy/automation-workers-robots-pandemic.html.

de Castella, T. April 20, 2012. "Are You a Luddite?" *BBC*. www.bbc.com/news/magazine-17770171.

Duszyński, M. April 27, 2022. "Gig Economy: Definition, Statistics & Trends [2022 Update]." Zety. https://zety.com/blog/gig-economy-statistics.

Roser, M., H. Ritchie, and E. Ortiz-Ospina. May 2019. "World Population Growth". OurWorldInData. https://ourworldindata.org/world-population-growth.

Space Foundation Editorial Team. April 1, 2020. "2019 Space Employment Hit 8-Year High, Launch Activity Reached Decade Growth of 39%, Research from the Space Report Q1 Analysis Shows." www.spacefoundation.org/2020/03/31.

Tappe, A. June 26, 2019. "Robots Could Take 20 Million Manufacturing Jobs by 2030." CNN. https://edition.cnn.com/2019/06/25/economy/robot-jobs-manufacturing-automation/index.html.

U.S. Department of Labor. September 22, 2020. "Employee Tenure Iin 2020." Washington, DC: Bureau of Labor Statistics, 2022. www.bls.gov/news.release/pdf/tenure.pdf.

UN Department of Economic and Social Affairs. June 17, 2019. "Growing at a Slower Pace, World Population Is Expected to Reach 9.7 Billion in 2050 and Could Peak at Nearly 11 Billion around 2100." www.un.org/development/desa/en/news/population/world-population-prospects-2019.html.

About the Author

Uma Vanka is a seasoned leader in business strategy consulting, specialized in transforming businesses and driving value through innovative deployment of technology. He is a tech enthusiast, keeping up with the ever-changing technology trends, and a futurist, specialized in business–technology integration. He is currently a partner within the strategy consulting group of Tata Consultancy Services. A former vice president at HCL Axon, he has played other high-profile roles at big names like Capgemini and NTT Data since 1999. He received a Bachelor of Engineering (Honors) degree from Birla Institute of Technology, India. He has authored several academic and professional publications and has been a career coach for hundreds of personnel.

Index

www.ingramcontent.com/pod-product-compliance
Lightning Source LLC
Chambersburg PA
CBHW061218220326
41599CB00025B/4679